NORTHROP N-63 *CONVOY FIGHTER*

THE NAVAL VTOL TURBOPROP TAILSITTER PROJECT OF 1950

Jared A. Zichek

RETROMECHANIX PRODUCTIONS

First published in the United States of America in 2015 by Jared A. Zichek, 2750 Torrey Pines Road, La Jolla, California 92037, USA

E-mail: editor@retromechanix.com

©2015 Jared A. Zichek

All rights reserved. All featured text and images are copyright 2015 their respective copyright holders. No part of this publication may be reproduced, stored in a retrieval system, or transmitted in any form by any means electronic, mechanical or otherwise without the written permission of the publisher.

ISBN: 978-0-9968754-1-7

www.retromechanix.com

All images in this publication are scanned from documents held by National Archives II, College Park, MD, RG 72 unless otherwise indicated. All color profile artwork is ©2015 Jared A. Zichek. Printed in USA.

Front Cover: Contemporary artist's impression of the Northrop N-63 convoy fighter proposal of 1950, one of the unsuccessful rivals to the Convair XFY-1 and Lockheed XFV-1. This artwork portrays a later version of the design from December 22, 1950. Below this is a speculative color profile of the N-63 in the overall Glossy Sea Blue scheme which was standard for most Navy aircraft in this period; it portrays the original configuration dating from November 6, 1950.

Note: Some of the images in this publication are not of ideal quality; however, they were the best available to the author at the time of publication. They are included due to their rarity and historical significance.

Introduction

The Northrop N-63 was one of five proposals submitted to the US Navy convoy fighter competition of 1950, which ultimately produced the Convair XFY-1 *Pogo* and Lockheed XFV-1 *Salmon*. Northrop was one of the three unsuccessful contenders, the others being Goodyear and Martin, whose proposals have been covered in previous volumes.

For those unfamiliar with the history of the concept, the idea of a turboprop tailsitter fighter emerged in the late 1940s, with the US Navy Bureau of Aeronautics (BuAer) beginning to seriously examine the feasibility of developing a vertical takeoff and landing (VTOL) tailsitter aircraft to protect convoys, task forces, and other vessels. These specialized interceptors would be placed on the decks of ships to provide a rapid defensive and reconnaissance capability until conventional carrier-based fighters could arrive and assist. The Battle of the Atlantic was fresh in the minds of Navy planners, who were concerned that the Soviets would engage in a similar campaign against merchant shipping if the nascent Cold War erupted into open conflict. BuAer's interest in a VTOL tailsitter fighter coincided with the development of new turboprop engines which provided enough horsepower to make the concept a reality.

BuAer's *Outline Specification for Class VF Airplane (Convoy Fighter) OS-122* was dated July 10, 1950. It listed the requirements for such an aircraft along with a scale demonstrator to verify the soundness of the concept. The document was distributed to the major aircraft manufacturers of the day, with the aforementioned companies responding in late November 1950. The products of this competition, the Convair XFY-1 and Lockheed XFV-1, never made it beyond the prototype stage, as they proved to be very difficult to land, suffered from power plant reliability issues, and were eclipsed in performance by contemporary jet fighters. The *Pogo* and *Salmon* became historical curiosities,

1) Cover to the Northrop N-63 convoy fighter proposal brochure dated November 6, 1950.

regularly making the list of world's worst/strangest aircraft; the VTOL turboprop tailsitter concept proved to be a dead end.

General Information

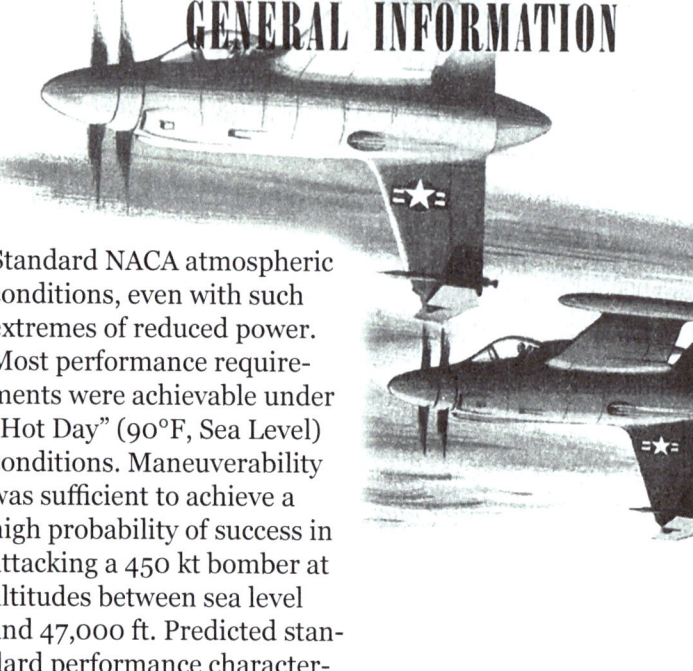

The N-63 convoy fighter proposal produced by Northrop Aircraft, Inc. of Hawthorne, California was dated November 6, 1950. It was a single-place high performance fighter designed to protect convoy vessels from attack by enemy aircraft, and for vertical unassisted takeoff from, and landings on, small platform areas afloat or ashore. It was capable of high performance and maneuverability at altitudes from sea level to a combat ceiling of 47,000 ft, and was controllable through a speed range from zero (hovering) to 528 kts.

The Northrop N-63 was a completely self-contained fighting weapon, requiring no auxiliary arresting or retrieving gear for successful takeoff and landing operations. It was designed for vertical takeoff from, and landing on, pitching and rolling decks under any sea and weather conditions in which normal operation of aircraft were expected. Shock absorbers at the aft extremity of the fuselage and at wing and vertical stabilizer tips, combined with widespread support points and a low center of gravity, permitted vertical landing even under the most severe conditions. Only small positioning dollies and simple tie-down provisions were required to locate and secure the airplane. It was in the ready-for-takeoff attitude at all times. Complete servicing and pre-flight operations were possible with the airplane in the vertical attitude.

Adequate control and stability during all phases of flight was assured by a full-powered control system, with autopilot stabilization during transition and hovering. Inherent level flight dynamic stability assured safe flight in the event of failure of either the autopilot or powered control system. Excellent pilot vision for both combat and search resulted from the location of the cockpit well forward of the wing. Pilot comfort was assured during all phases of flight. A rotatable pilot's seat permitted excellent vision down and aft during hovering and landing operations. Full control of the airplane was possible at any attitude, with or without autopilot operation.

An Allison XT-40-A-8 turboprop engine drove an Aeroproducts 15.5 ft six-blade dual-rotation propeller. Four 20 mm aircraft guns with 600 rounds of ammunition were mounted in easily accessible wingtip pods. The Mk 6 gunsight and either APG-37, APG-25, or APS-25 radar provided accurate fire control.

Performance in all respects met and in many cases exceeded specification requirements. Whereas only safe horizontal flight was required with one power unit of the XT-40-A-8 inoperative, the Northrop design permitted hovering and successful landing, under Standard NACA atmospheric conditions, even with such extremes of reduced power. Most performance requirements were achievable under "Hot Day" (90°F, Sea Level) conditions. Maneuverability was sufficient to achieve a high probability of success in attacking a 450 kt bomber at altitudes between sea level and 47,000 ft. Predicted standard performance characteristics included:

Rate of climb at sea level:	11,270 ft/min
Combat ceiling:	47,000 ft
Maximum speed:	528 kts
Endurance:	2.78 hours
Combat radius:	428 nm

Design History

The Northrop N-63 convoy fighter configuration evolved as the logical result of efforts to derive an optimum design to meet the various requirements set forth in the proposed specification. With the primary mission defined and certain components specified by Navy preference, analytical studies and years of Northrop experience designing full-power control systems and stable unconventional aircraft platforms were combined to produce the best possible vertically-rising convoy fighter.

Initial studies indicated that a tractor, dual-rotation propeller offered the most promise and that a two-speed reduction gear was necessary to achieve maximum propeller efficiency over a great range of speed. Preliminary analyses indicated that autopilot stabilization during hovering was required, although manual control could have been provided in the event of autopilot failure. Northrop experience indicated that a variation of control forces and reliability of operation made mandatory a fully powered control system.

Two general types of configuration were considered in the initial studies. One approach assumed an

2-3) Title and Table of Contents pages from the Northrop N-63 brochure depicting the aircraft performing its primary mission—protecting a convoy of merchant vessels.

CONVOY FIGHTER VF

NORTHROP AIRCRAFT INC. HAWTHORNE, CALIFORNIA

MODEL N-63

BROCHURE NO. 32　　　　　　　　　　　COPY NO.

NOVEMBER 6, 1950

CONTENTS

1. GENERAL INFORMATION
2. DESIGN HISTORY
3. READY FOR TAKE-OFF
4. N-63 IN FLIGHT
5. TACTICAL VERSATILITY
6. APPROACHING FOR A LANDING
7. AIRPLANE STOWAGE
8. GENERAL ARRANGEMENT
9. INBOARD PROFILE
10. N-63 TRANSPARENT PERSPECTIVE
11. DESCRIPTIVE DATA
12. PERFORMANCE SUMMARY
13. PERFORMANCE CHARTS
14. PERFORMANCE NOTES
15. PRODUCTION BREAKDOWN
16. ENGINE REMOVAL AND MAINTENANCE
17. ARMAMENT AND LANDING GEAR DETAIL
18. FUEL SYSTEM
19. FLIGHT CONTROL SYSTEM
20. AUTO PILOT SYSTEM

ENGINEERING DRAWINGS

21. WING STRUCTURE
22. FUSELAGE STRUCTURE
23. EMPENNAGE STRUCTURE
24. LANDING GEAR
25. FUEL SYSTEM DIAGRAM
26. POWER PLANT INSTALLATION
27. EXTERNAL ANTENNA LOCATION
28. CONTROL SYSTEM
29. ARMAMENT INSTALLATION
30. PILOT'S SEAT
31. HYDRAULIC SYSTEM DIAGRAM

essentially conventional airplane to be recovered by a shipboard retrieving mechanism designed to meet the various requirements imposed by such a design. Studies indicated that such a retrieving gear would have been complicated and required an elaborate shipboard installation.

The other basic approach undertook the development of an unconventional airplane which was landed vertically, with simultaneous development of a matching retrieving gear which permitted the design of both components to be most effective. This retrieving gear was less complicated than the other and involved less elaborate shipboard installation.

Several wing planforms were considered, including swept, delta and thin straight wings. Theoretical studies substantiated by test of a Navy model at the David Taylor Model Basin indicated that wings with any appreciable degree of sweepback became highly unstable at low speed and high engine power. A thin straight wing was therefore selected in preference to the less stable swept or delta planforms.

Comprehensive studies of the effects of Mach number and power variations upon longitudinal stability were conducted. General results of these investigations led to the conclusion that (1) a propeller and wing arrangement could be designed with small changes in stability due to Mach number or power effects, but that (2) the addition of a conventionally located horizontal tail would cause large and erratic stability and trim shifts. The possibilities of buffeting or shake were greatly increased by the strong propeller slipstream. An unconventional location for the horizontal tail was indicated as the solution.

Intensive investigations of landing systems took into account various trapezes, barriers, nets, clamshells, booms and arresting hooks. The problem finally resolved itself into rather simple terms which led to the system finally selected as the most effective and simplest means of retrieving the airplane.

A successful landing system required compatibility with some reasonable positioning error of the airplane. In order to maintain stability in hovering during the final phases of the landing, it appeared extremely undesirable to attach any restraint to the airplane before its weight rested fully upon the retrieving gear. Thus, the problem of retrieving became merely one of transferring support of the airplane's weight from the propeller to the retrieving mechanism quickly and positively. It followed that the most desirable and effective landing system would simply have the airplane alight upright on a flat landing platform without any auxiliary arresting or retrieving mechanism. Loads imposed by descent velocities, rolling and pitching of the ship, and misalignment of the airplane could be absorbed by properly designed shock struts, while upsetting after contact could be prevented by widely spacing the support points.

Aerodynamic and structural investigations indicated that a conventional empennage was undesirable. Relocation of the empennage permitted the airplane to be supported on its wing tips in the vertical attitude and eliminated the erratic effects of downwash on the horizontal tail. Directional stability was provided by the addition of a large ventral vertical fin, which also served as the necessary third landing support. The remaining problem of providing satisfactory longitudinal trim and control was solved by adding a movable horizontal surface at the bottom of the vertical fin, away from both wing wake and propeller slipstream.

As a result of these various studies, the desirable characteristics of an optimum configuration emerged. Stability and control requirements dictated a thin straight wing. Location of gun pods at the tips of the straight wing permitted good gun-platform characteristics without the dangers of aeroelastic twist and deflection associated with swept wings. The unconventional ventral fin and horizontal tail provided satisfactory stability and trim characteristics. Wide spread landing support points were provided at wing and fin tips, thus simplifying shipboard installations. Adequate control surface area would be located in the propeller slipstream for control during hovering flight.

Note: The remainder of the Northrop N-63 convoy fighter brochure is shown over the next 17 pages. Due to the tight integration of text and graphics in the original images, the majority of it is reproduced unaltered without additional captions.

READY FOR TAKE-OFF

The Northrop Convoy Fighter is a self-contained fighting weapon requiring a minimum of deck or ground handling facilities. It can operate from a simple flat deck over the stern of a ship, or from any equivalent flat area. Only small positioning dollies and simple tie-down provisions are required for locating and securing the airplane. It requires no special hoisting apparatus since it is in the take-off attitude at all times.

N-63 IN FLIGHT

Excellent visibility, aerodynamic cleanness and good gun-platform stability make the Northrop Convoy Fighter an effective fighting weapon. The pilot's cockpit has been placed much farther forward than in more conventional fighters. As a result visibility forward and down, to the sides, aft and overhead are exceptionally good.

Simplicity of design and configuration fineness permit a wide range of forward speeds from zero (hovering) to 528 knots. Four 20 mm. guns mounted in pods at the tips of the straight wings provide heavy fire-power coupled with the ultimate in accuracy of fire control. The line of fire of each gun is well outboard of the propeller circles.

TACTICAL VERSATILITY

The Northrop Convoy Fighter, though designed primarily for convoy protection, is well suited to the additional demands which might be made of it by Amphibious Ground Forces. Its unique tail landing gear gives real meaning to the heretofore academic phrase: "Close Ground Support."

APPROACHING FOR A LANDING

The Northrop Convoy Fighter is designed to land vertically on a flat deck over the stern of a ship, or on any equivalent flat area afloat or ashore. The airplane is placed in the hovering attitude over the platform, then lowered until it rests on the deck. Fine positive control in the hovering position makes the entire landing operation routine. Landing is accomplished with a minimum of deck gear or equipment. No arresting or retrieving gear is necessary.

The wide tread of the tail landing shock absorbers permits completely self-contained landing on pitching and rolling decks under the worst possible weather conditions in which the airplane might be operated. This completely self-contained operation of the airplane is an outstanding tactical advantage.

N-63 STOWAGE

The airplane has been designed to be stowed or serviced in the vertical attitude to eliminate bulky handling equipment. In this attitude, the stability of the airplane at rest is greater than it would be if it were secured on equipment provided for horizontal stowage. This characteristic is directly attributable to the wide tread of the tail landing gear and the proximity of the center of gravity to the deck.

Tie-down cables, easily attached and removed, are provided to secure the airplane. Covers for propellers, canopy, etc., are provided for use in unfavorable weather. A dolly under each of the three landing struts is used for maneuvering the airplane on deck. The main central shock absorber is locked in the static position when the airplane is to be moved about.

N-63 GENERAL ARRANGEMENT

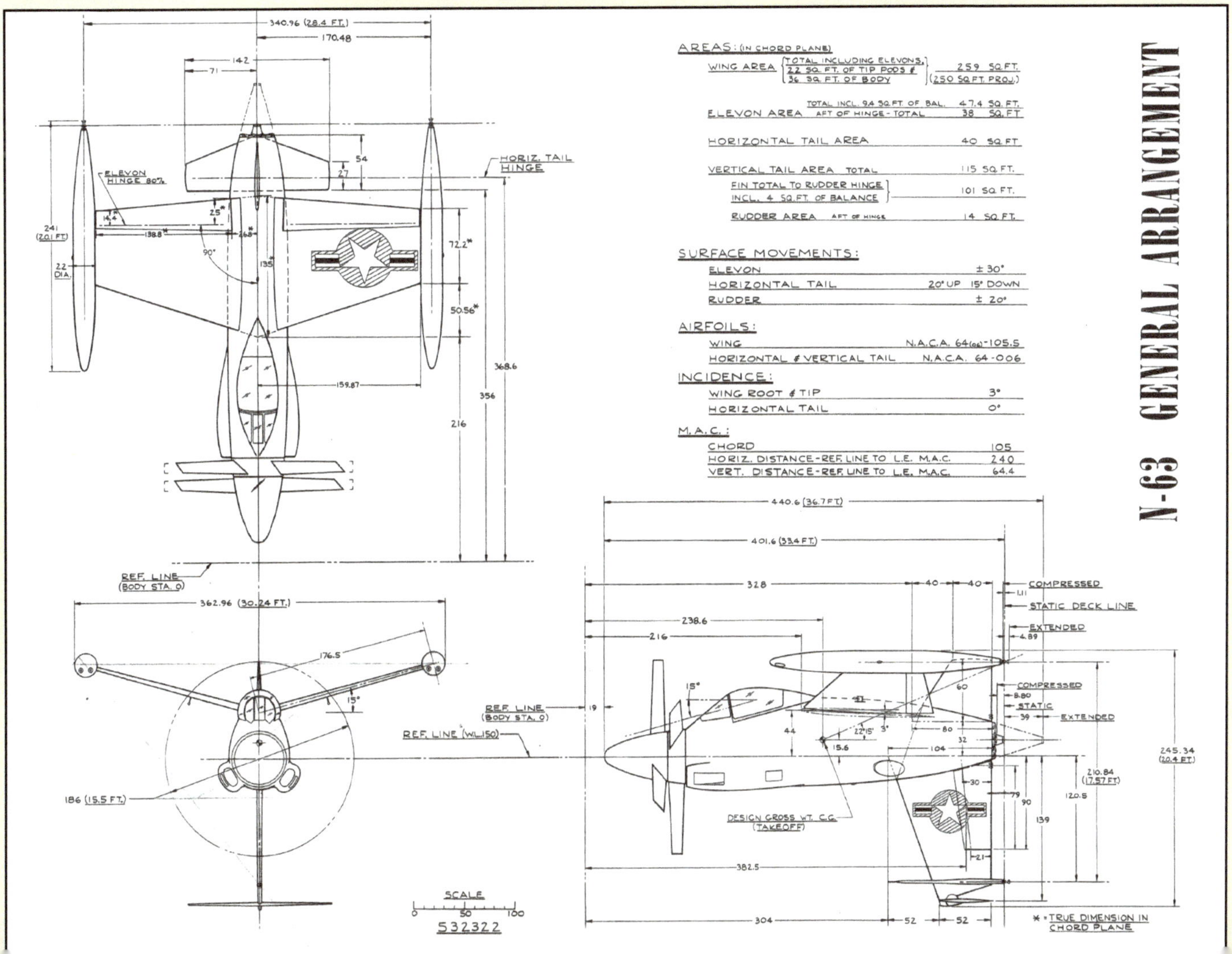

AREAS: (IN CHORD PLANE)

WING AREA	TOTAL INCLUDING ELEVONS, 22 SQ. FT. OF TIP PODS & 36 SQ FT. OF BODY	259 SQ. FT. (250 SQ FT. PROJ.)
ELEVON AREA	TOTAL INCL. 9.4 SQ FT OF BAL.	47.4 SQ. FT.
	AFT OF HINGE - TOTAL	38 SQ FT
HORIZONTAL TAIL AREA		40 SQ FT
VERTICAL TAIL AREA	TOTAL	115 SQ. FT.
	FIN TOTAL TO RUDDER HINGE INCL. 4 SQ.FT. OF BALANCE	101 SQ FT.
	RUDDER AREA AFT OF HINGE	14 SQ FT.

SURFACE MOVEMENTS:

ELEVON	± 30°
HORIZONTAL TAIL	20° UP 15° DOWN
RUDDER	± 20°

AIRFOILS:

WING	N.A.C.A. 64(a)-105.5
HORIZONTAL & VERTICAL TAIL	N.A.C.A. 64-006

INCIDENCE:

WING ROOT & TIP	3°
HORIZONTAL TAIL	0°

M.A.C.:

CHORD	105
HORIZ. DISTANCE - REF. LINE TO L.E. M.A.C.	240
VERT. DISTANCE - REF. LINE TO L.E. M.A.C.	64.4

* = TRUE DIMENSION IN CHORD PLANE

N-63 TRANSPARENT PERSPECTIVE

DESCRIPTIVE DATA

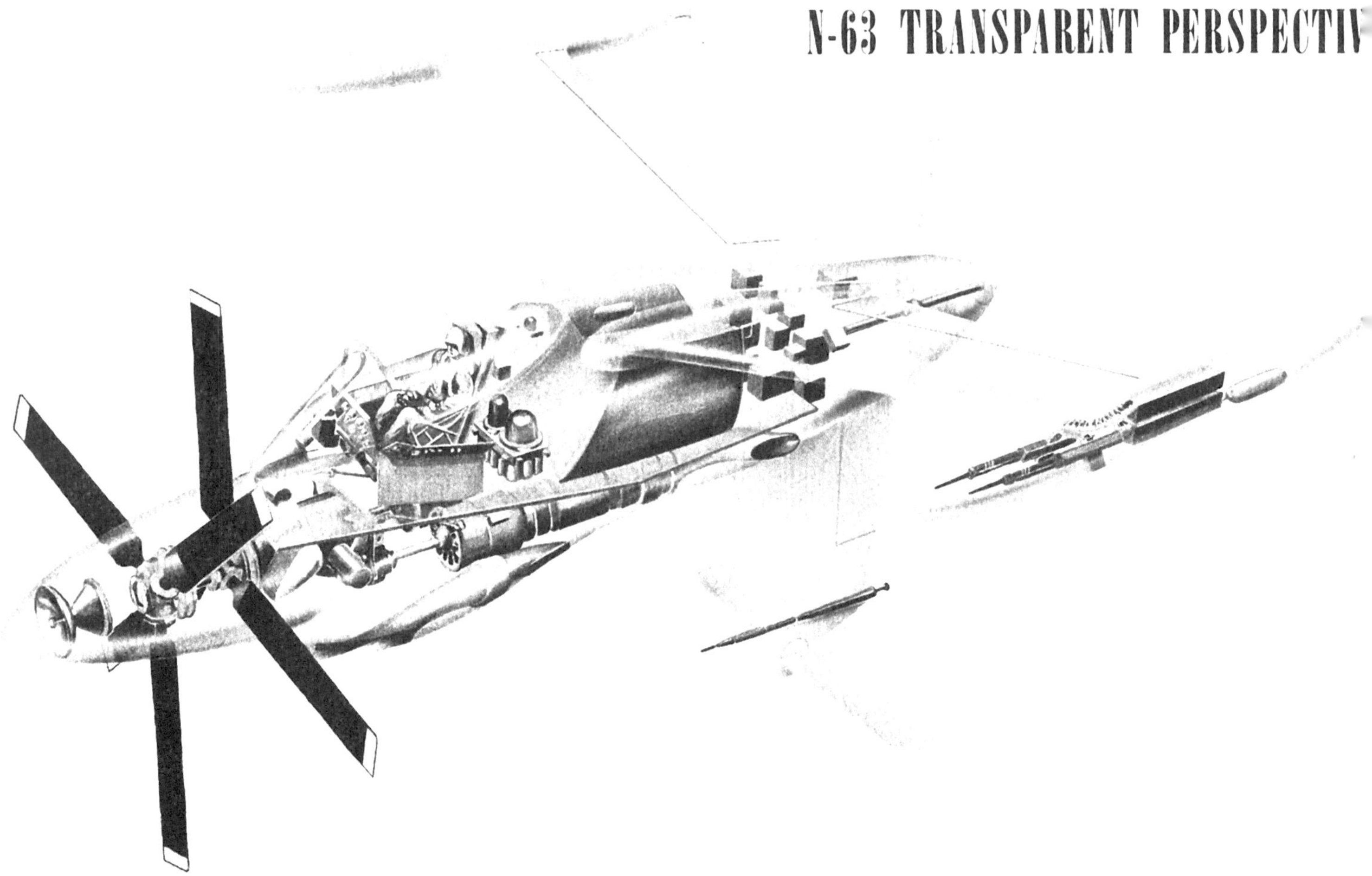

MISSION AND DESCRIPTION

The primary mission of the Northrop N-63 airplane is to protect convoy vessels from air attack by enemy aircraft.

The Northrop N-63 is a proposed U.S. Navy Class VF (Convoy Fighter) Airplane based on BuAer Outline Specification OS-122. It is designed for vertical unassisted take-off from, and landing on, small platform areas of convoy vessels. It also is designed for high performance at low and medium altitudes and for operation under all weather conditions.

The airplane is essentially a conventional single-engine tractor monoplane configuration except for features appropriate to vertical take-off and landing. Longitudinal control at low speed and lateral control for all conditions are obtained by elevons, which are drooped to improve ceiling and maneuverability. Longitudinal control during normal flight at higher speeds is obtained by an all-movable horizontal tail. Directional control is provided by a rudder on the vertical tail. Aerodynamic braking is provided by the propeller alone. The alighting gear consists of a main central shock absorber in the tail and stabilizer shock absorbers on the wing tips and lower fin tip. Construction is all-metal. Crew consists of a pilot.

DIMENSIONS

Span	30.2 ft.
Length	33.4 ft.
Height	20.4 ft.°
Wing Area	250. sq.ft.

°In horizontal position

WEIGHTS

Loading	Pounds	L.F.
Empty	12,283 (E)	
Basic	12,801 (E)	
Design (flight)	15,600	7.5
Combat	15,454 (E)	7.5
Max. Take-off	16,780 (E)°	
Max. Landing	14,795 (E)	

°Limited by Space

FUEL AND OIL

Location	No. Tanks	Cap.
Fuselage	1°	552.5 gal.
Total		552.5 gal.
Spec.		MIL-F-5572
Grade		100/130

°Not self-sealing

OIL

Capacity (1 fus. tank)	7.5 gal.
Spec.	MIL-O-6086
Grade	M

ELECTRONICS

UHF Trans-receiver	AN/ARC-27
Homing Receiver	AN/ARR-2A
Radio Altimeter	AN/APN-22
Gun-laying Radar	AN/APG-37
Radar Identification	AN/APX-6

POWER PLANT

ENGINE

Number & Model	(1) XT40-A-8
Manufacturer	Allison
Type	axial-flow turbo-prop.
Augmentation	None
Length	190 in.
Width	43 in.
Height	35 in.
Reduction gear	
Take-off (& landing)	10.95:1
Normal	15.67:1
Specification	272-B
	(31 May 1950)

PROPELLER

Manufacturer	Aeroproducts
No. blades/dia.	6/15.5 ft.
Propeller No.	AD86564F

RATING

(Sea level static guarantees)

	Engine rpm	Shaft Power bhp	Jet Thrust lb	Fuel Cons. lb/hr	Time Limit min.
Take-off*	15,700	6825	1685	4325**	5
Military*	14,300	6955	1363	4095**	30
Normal	14,000	5790	1225	3642**	

*Military rating used for take-off and landing.
**Using Grade JP-3 (Spec. MIL-F-5624) fuel.

ARMAMENT

No. & cal of guns	(4) 20-mm
Amm. per gun	150 rds.

IN TRANSITION BEFORE LANDING

PERFORMANCE SUMMARY

LOADING CONDITION		OUTLINE SPEC. OS-122 MISSION		NAVY F-1 MISSION	NAVY F-5 MISSION	FERRY MISSION
Take-off weight	lb.	16,780		16,780	16,780	16,780
Fuel	lb.	3,315		3,315	3,315	3,315
Bombs	lb.	None		None	None	None
Wing/Power loading (A)	lb/sq.ft; lb/bhp	67.1/2.41		67.1/2.41	67.1/2.41	67.1/2.41
Disc loading (A)	lb/sq.ft.	88.9		88.9	88.9	88.9
Stall speed—Power off	kn.	143		143	143	143
Stall speed—Power off - No fuel	kn.	128		128	128	128
Stall speed—Power on	kn.	106		106	106	106
Maximum speed/alt (B)	kn/ft.	508/22,000		508/22,000	508/22,000	508/22,000
Take-off distance	ft.	0		0	0	0
Rate of climb — sea level (B)	ft/min.	8350		8350	8350	8350
Service ceiling (B)	ft.	44,700		44,700	44,700	44,700
Time-to-climb 20,000 ft. (C)	min.	2.6		2.6	2.6	2.6
Time-to-climb 30,000 ft. (C)	min.	4.5		4.5	4.5	4.5
Vertical rate of climb - sea level (C)	ft/min.	7470		7470	7470	7470
Absolute hovering ceiling (C)	ft.	8900		8900	8900	8900
Combat range/V av	n.mi/kn.	—		1085/402	1085/402	1085/402
Combat radius/V av	n.mi/kn.	—		390/400	428/401	—
Total endurance/V av-35,000 ft.	hr/kn.	2.95/333		—	—	—
LOADING CONDITION		COMBAT		COMBAT	COMBAT	FINAL CRUISE
Gross weight	lb.	15,454		14,790	14,740	13,797
Engine power		Max.	Normal	Maximum	Maximum	Maximum
Fuel	lb.	1989		1525	1479	332
Bombs/Tanks		None		None	None	None
Max. speed at sea level	kn.	510	483	510	510	510
Max. speed/alt	kn/ft	528/21,000	509/23,000	529/21,000	529/21,000	530/22,000
Combat speed/Alt	kn/ft	512/35,000	500/35,000	527/15,000	515/35,000	513/37,200
Rate of climb at sea level	ft/min.	11,270	9220	11,850	11,900	12,750
Rate of climb/Alt	ft/min/ft.	4140/35,000	3330/35,000	8610/15,000	4430/35,000	4200/37,200
Combat ceiling (500 fpm)	ft.	47,000	—	48,000	48,100	49,400
Service ceiling (B)	ft.	—	46,600	47,300	47,400	48,900
Service ceiling (C)	ft.	48,300	—	49,300	49,400	50,800
Time-to-climb/Alt.	min/ft.	5.2/35,000	—	4.8/35,000	4.8/35,000	4.3/35,000
Landing weight	lb.	13,416		13,389	13,389	13,389
Landing distance	ft.	0		0	0	0

NOTES
(A) Shaft power at sea level
(B) Normal power
(C) Maximum power

PERFORMANCE SUMMARY

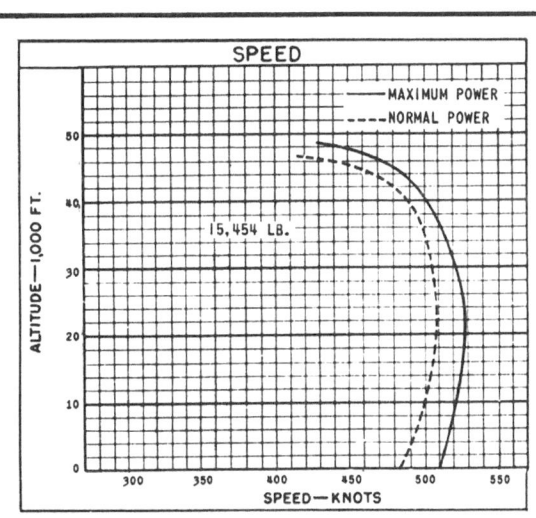
SPEED

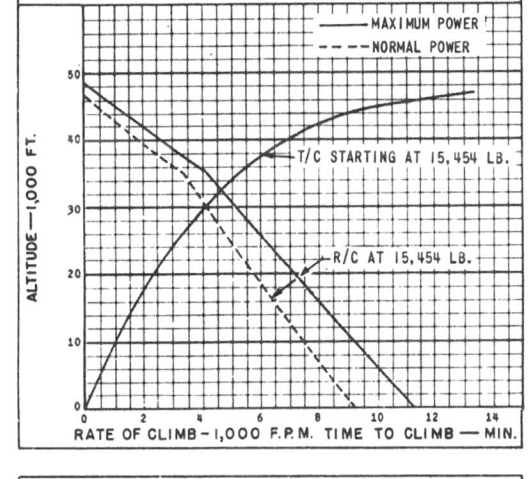
CLIMB

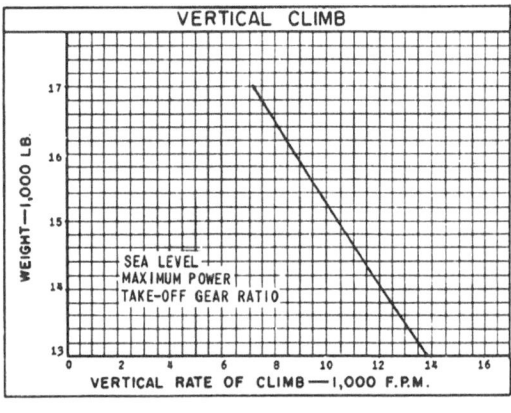
VERTICAL CLIMB

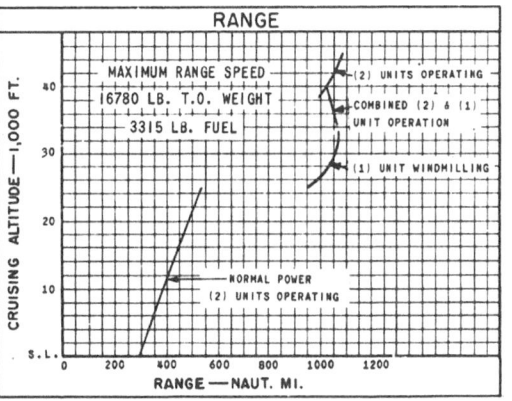
RANGE

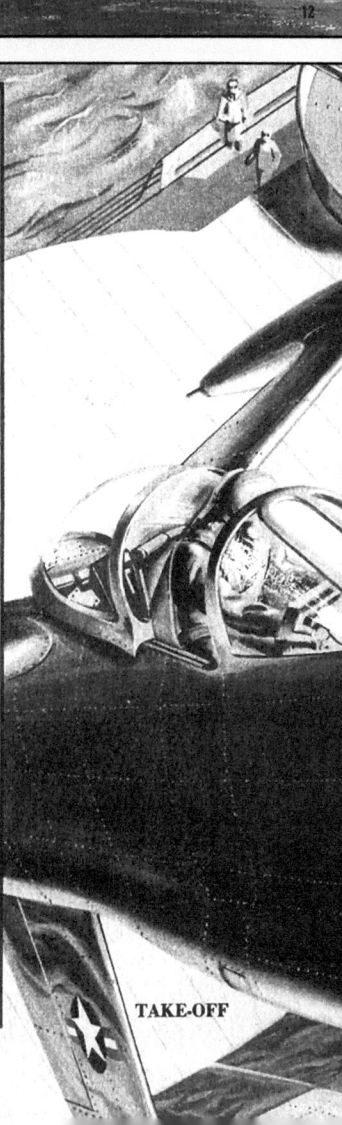

PERFORMANCE CHARTS

NOTES

(a) **Performance basis:**
  (1) NACA standard conditions, no wind, single aircraft.
  (2) Calculated airplane and propeller characteristics; estimated and guaranteed engine characteristics.
  (3) Blade thickness/chord ratio = 0.0497 at 0.7 radius

(b) **Endurance, range, and radii are based on Allison Specification 272-B (as revised 31 May 1950) fuel consumption data pertaining to Grade JP-3 fuel (Specification MIL-F-5624) with a density of 6.5 lb/gal.**

(c) **Fuel consumption data are increased 5 per cent.**

(d) **Mission flight plans:**
  (1) Navy Outline Specification OS-122 mission:
    1. Take-off fuel allowance ≡ 5 min. at maximum power at sea level.
    2. Climb to 35,000 ft. at military power.
    3. Loiter for 130 min. at 35,000 ft. at maximum-endurance speed (one power unit windmilling).
    4. Cruise out 100 n. mi. at 35,000 ft. at maximum power.
    5. Combat 3 min. at 35,000 ft. at military power.
    6. Cruise back at maximum-range speed, starting at 37,400 ft. and ending at 37,700 ft. (one power unit windmilling).
    7. Approach and landing fuel allowance ≡ 5 min. at static military power at sea level.

  (2) Navy Basic Fighter F-4 mission (radius):
    1. Take-off fuel allowance ≡ 5 min. at normal power at sea level.
    2. Climb to 44,300 ft. at maximum power.
    3. Cruise out at long-range speed, arriving over target at 45,500 ft.
    4. Descend to 15,000 ft. and combat for 10 min. at maximum power.*
    5. Climb to 36,600 ft. at maximum power.
    6. Cruise back at long-range speed (one power unit windmilling), arriving over base at 37,800 ft.
    7. Reserve ≡ 10% of initial fuel.

  (3) Navy Basic Fighter F-4 mission (range):
    1. Take-off fuel allowance ≡ 5 min. at normal power at sea level.
    2. Climb to 44,300 ft. at maximum power.
    3. Cruise at long range speed (two units operating).
    4. Descend to cruise altitude for one unit windmilling.
    5. Cruise at long range speed, (one unit windmilling), arriving over destination at 37,200 ft.
    6. Reserve ≡ 10% of initial fuel.

  (4) Navy Basic Fighter F-5 mission (radius):
    Same as Navy F-4 mission (radius) except:
    3. Cruise out at long-range speed, arriving over target at 45,500 ft.
    4. Descend to 35,000 ft. and combat for 15 min. at maximum power.*
    5. Climb to 36,500 ft. at maximum power.

  (5) Navy Basic Fighter F-5 mission (range):
    Same as Navy F-4 mission (range).

  (6) Ferry mission:
    Same as Navy F-4 mission (range).

(e) **When Grade 100/130 fuel (Specification MIL-F-5572) is used, fuel consumption is reduced 2 per cent and endurance, range, and radii are correspondingly increased.**

* No fuel nor distance allowed for descent.
  No distance allowed for combat.

PRODUCTION BREAK DOWN

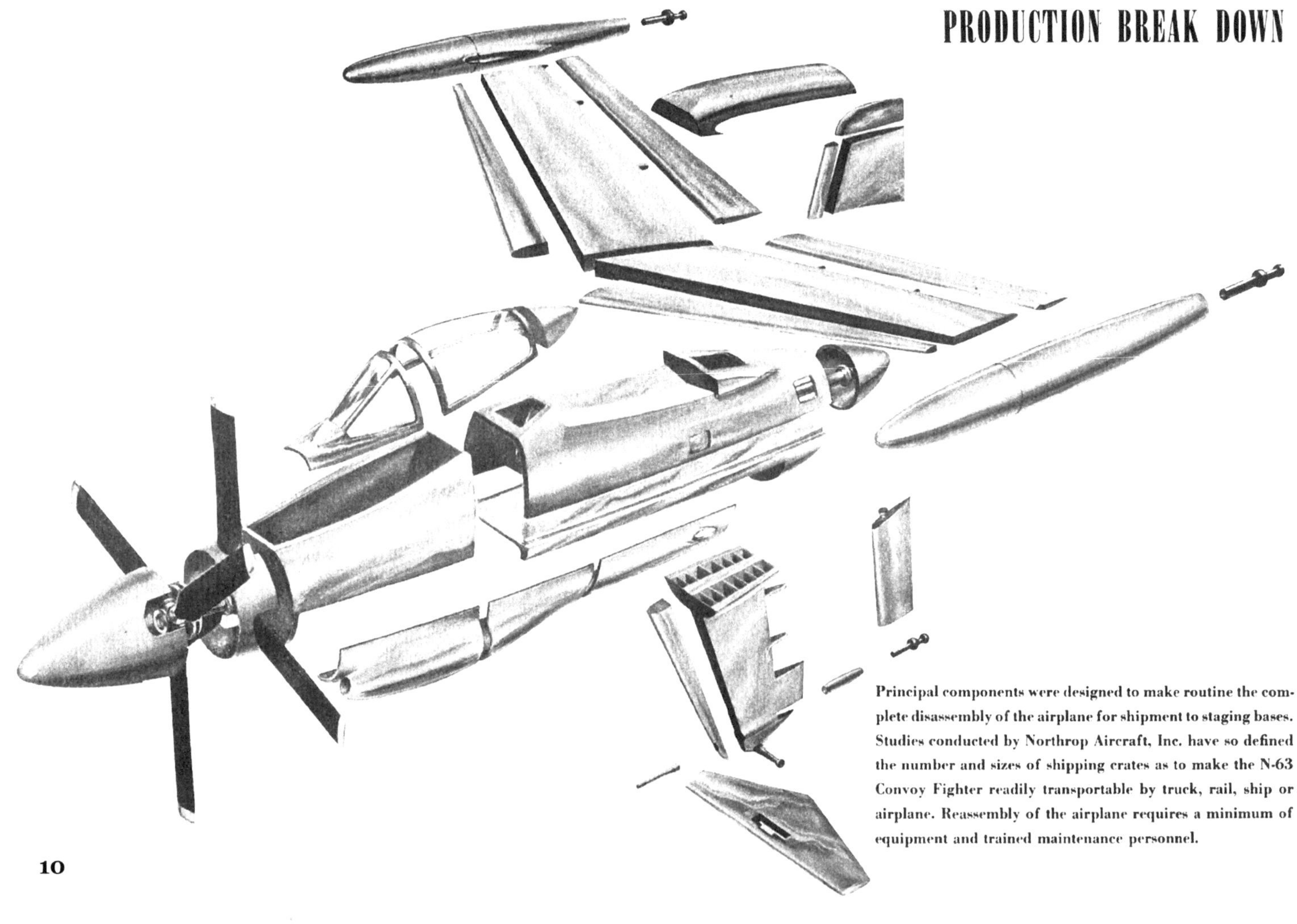

Principal components were designed to make routine the complete disassembly of the airplane for shipment to staging bases. Studies conducted by Northrop Aircraft, Inc. have so defined the number and sizes of shipping crates as to make the N-63 Convoy Fighter readily transportable by truck, rail, ship or airplane. Reassembly of the airplane requires a minimum of equipment and trained maintenance personnel.

ENGINE REMOVAL AND MAINTENANCE

Engine maintenance and removal may be accomplished with the airplane in the vertical attitude. Removal of three panels on the bottom of the fuselage permits complete servicing of the engine. To remove the engine from the airframe, it is necessary to remove the propellers and spinner, and disconnect the air ducts and lines. The power plant installation has been designed to facilitate this operation by minimizing the time requirements.

On shipboard, a portable hoist taking power from the ship's hoist may be rigged to support the engine. Ashore, any standard hoist of adequate (27 Ft.) capacity may be employed.

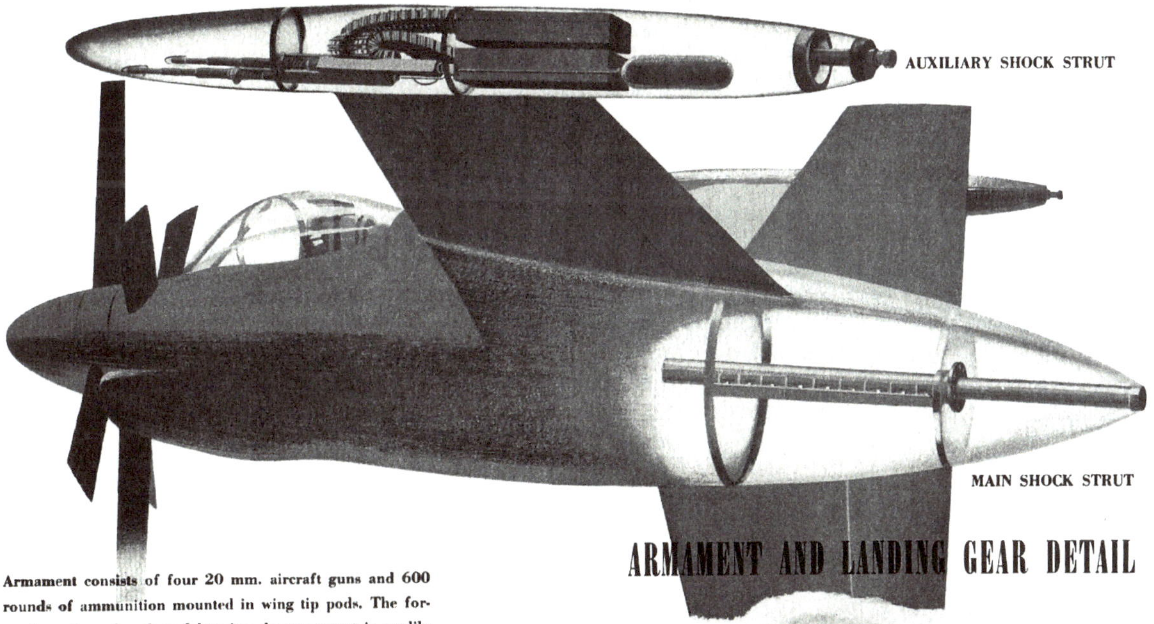

ARMAMENT AND LANDING GEAR DETAIL

Armament consists of four 20 mm. aircraft guns and 600 rounds of ammunition mounted in wing tip pods. The forward portion of each pod housing the armament is readily removable and completely interchangeable except for bore sighting the guns. Large access doors are provided for servicing and weapon adjustment.

The landing gear for the Northrop Convoy Fighter consists of a central main shock strut in the tail of the airplane, two stabilizing shock struts in the aft section of the wing tip pods and one stabilizing shock strut extending aft of the lower vertical stabilizer. The central shock strut is contained in a flexible non-metallic housing designed to collapse with the strut. This strut may be locked in the static (partially collapsed) position when moving the airplane about on deck dollies.

AUXILIARY SHOCK STRUT

MAIN SHOCK STRUT

ARMAMENT POD REMOVAL

FUEL SYSTEM

The [illegible] fuel system consists of a single fuselage tank and sump with a total usable capacity of 552 gallons. Boost pumps in the tank and sump supply 90 per cent of the usable fuel to the engine at all level flight attitudes and 99 per cent of the usable fuel during hovering.

The tank system is vented to prevent excessive bursting or collapsing bladder cell pressures. At flight altitudes where the fuel normally boils, a suction-pressure relief valve in the vent line closes. Fuel boiling thus serves merely to pressurize the system and keeps fuel losses to a minimum.

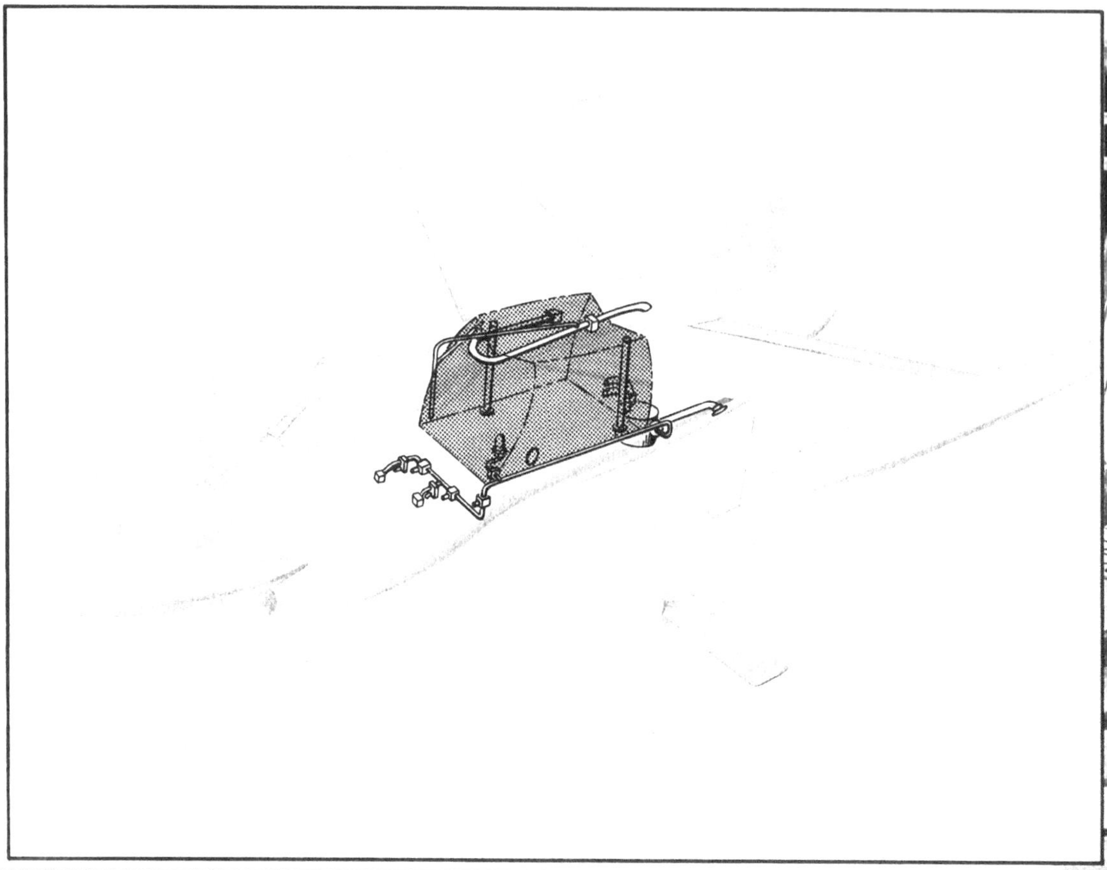

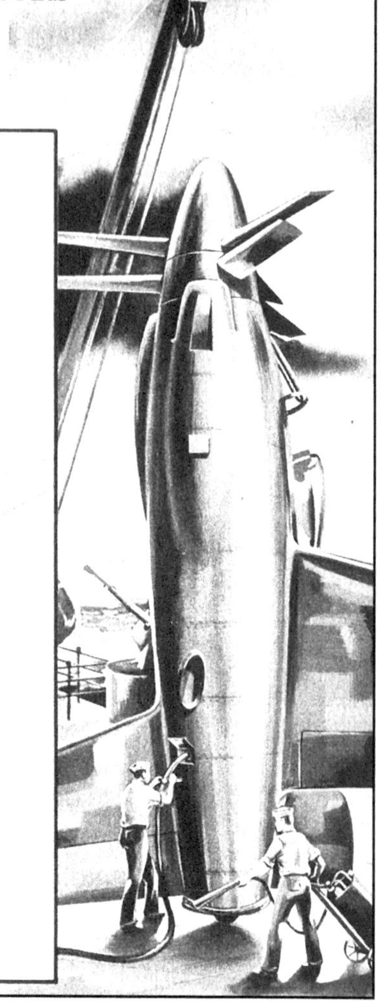

FLIGHT CONTROL SYSTEM

Control during hovering, transition, and take-off and landing is provided by elevons and rudder located in the propeller slipstream. Roll and pitch control are provided by the elevons, while the rudder contributes yaw control. In horizontal flight, elevator action of the elevons is eliminated and they become conventional ailerons. Directional control is provided by the rudder, while longitudinal control is provided by the horizontal tail located safely away from the wing wake and propeller slipstream. The Northrop fully powered system assures full control during all phases of flight.

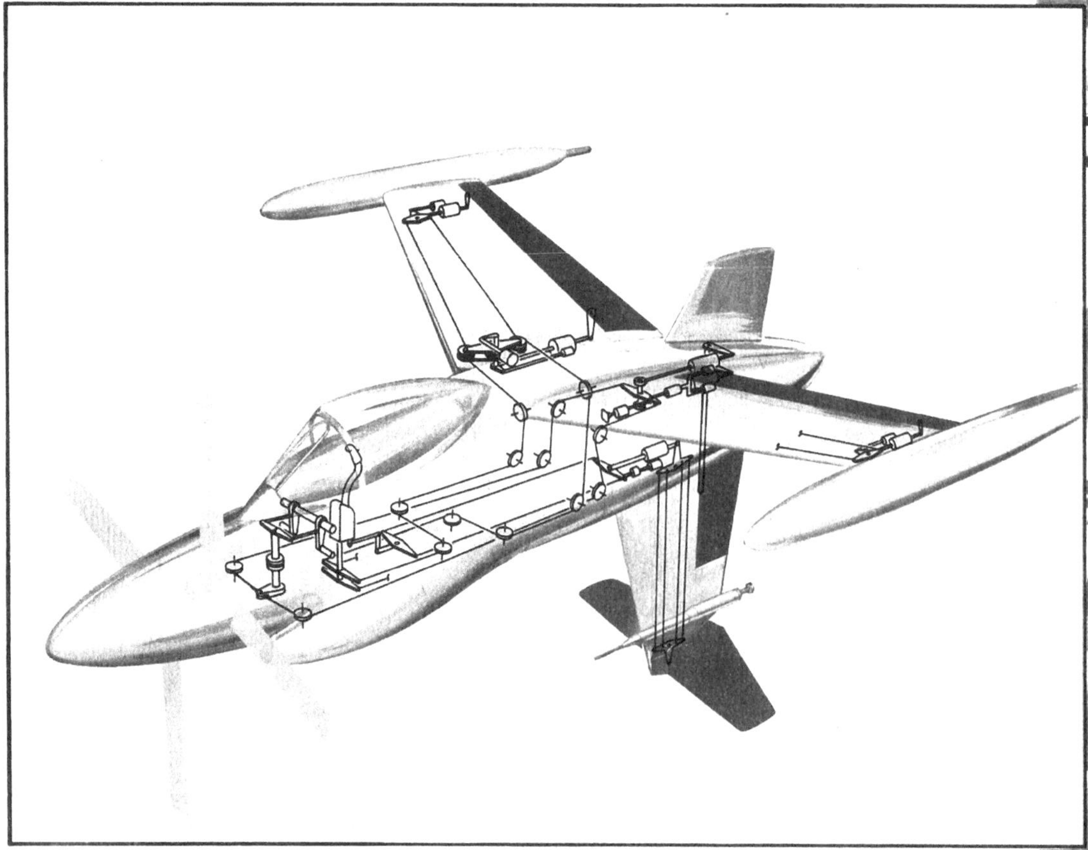

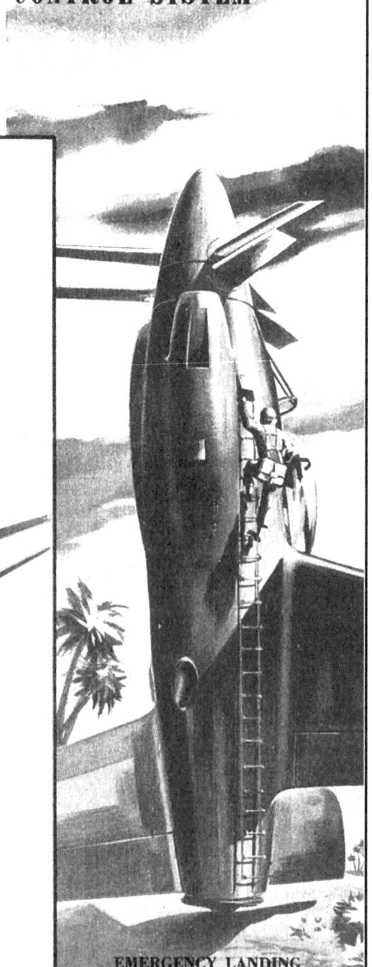

EMERGENCY LANDING

The normal flight autopilot (in blue) controls longitudinal motions by means of an accelerometer working through the elevators (elevons). Zero side slip is maintained by a lateral accelerometer working through the rudder. Roll stabilization is achieved by means of a roll rate gyro and integrator working through the ailerons (elevons). Direction reference is the G-2 compass. Automatic elevon droop for high G turns is an inherent part of the autopilot. The hovering autopilot uses the components shown in black. The autopilot is aerobatic and control is maintained through the stick and rudder pedals alone. Rudder and aileron actuators double as trimmers.

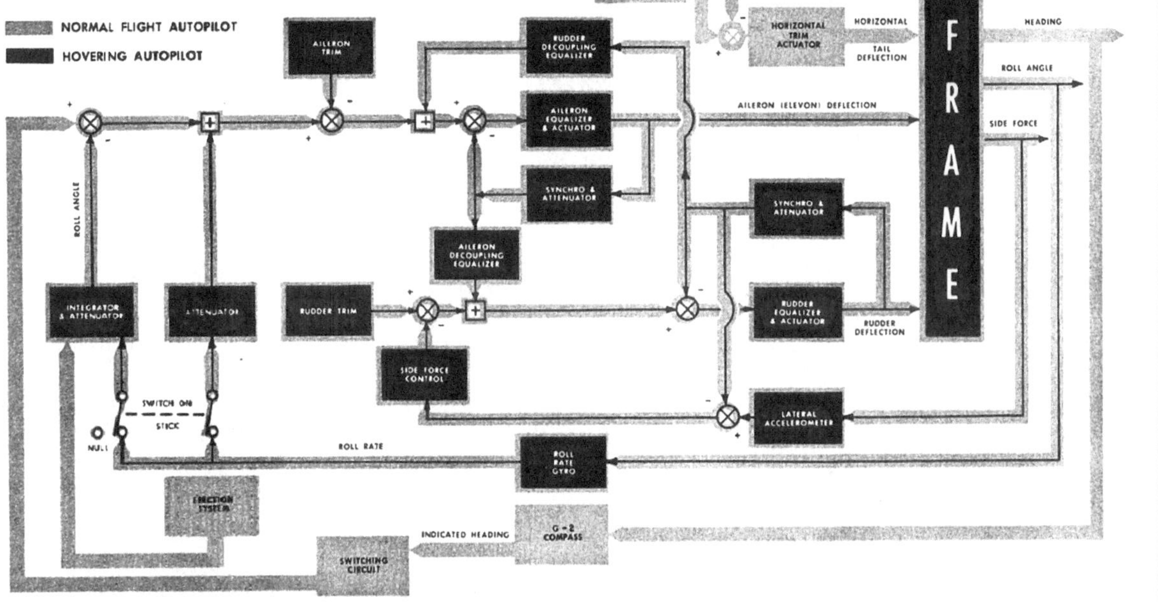

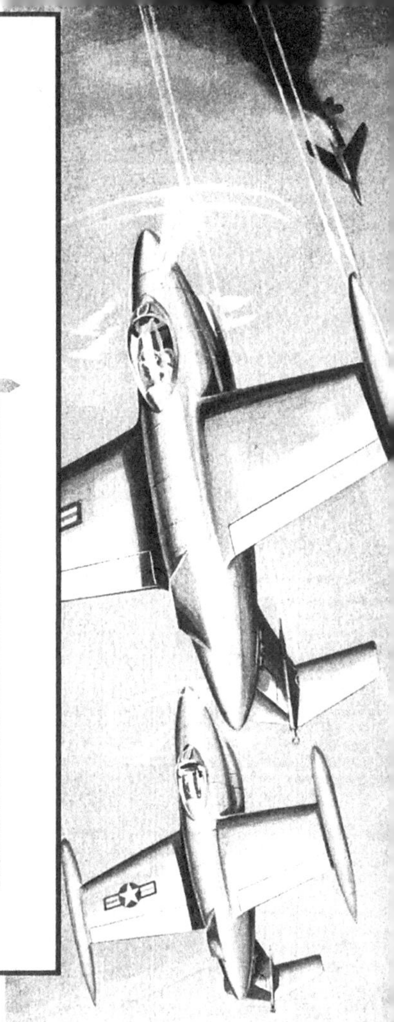

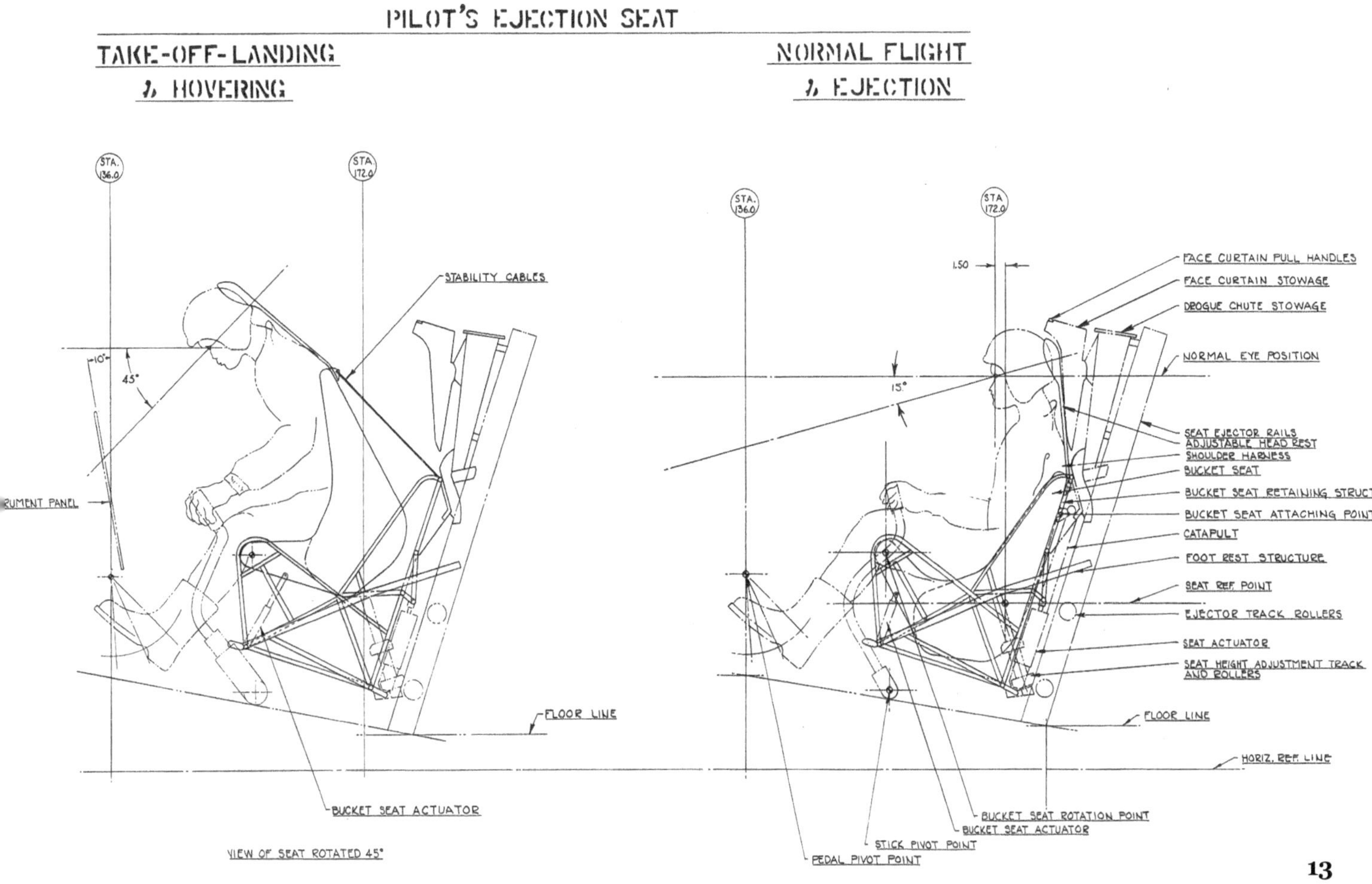

■ NORMAL FLIGHT AUTOPILOT
■ HOVERING AUTOPILOT

PILOT'S EJECTION SEAT

TAKE-OFF-LANDING & HOVERING

NORMAL FLIGHT & EJECTION

13

4) Inboard profile of the Northrop N-63 convoy fighter showing the location of the major internal components. (Please note that the layout of this and other blueprints in this book has been altered to better fit the format of the publication).

5) Structural diagram of the N-63's aluminum alloy fuselage, which was of semi-monocoque construction.

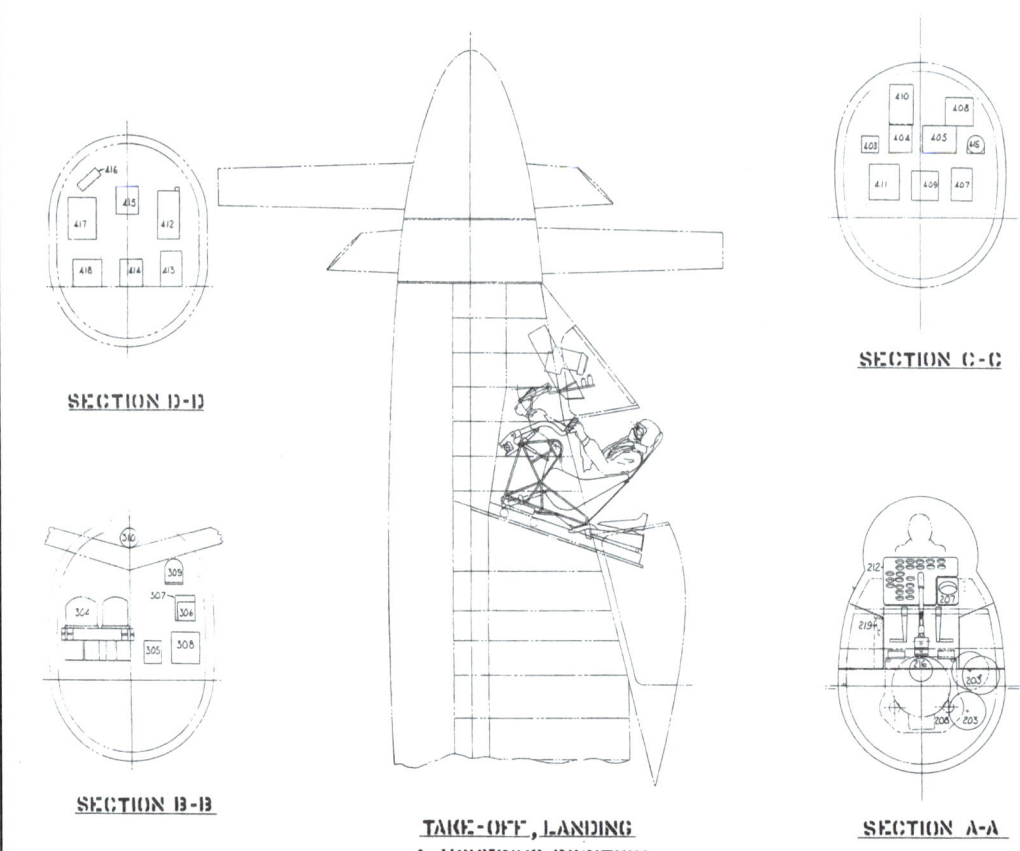

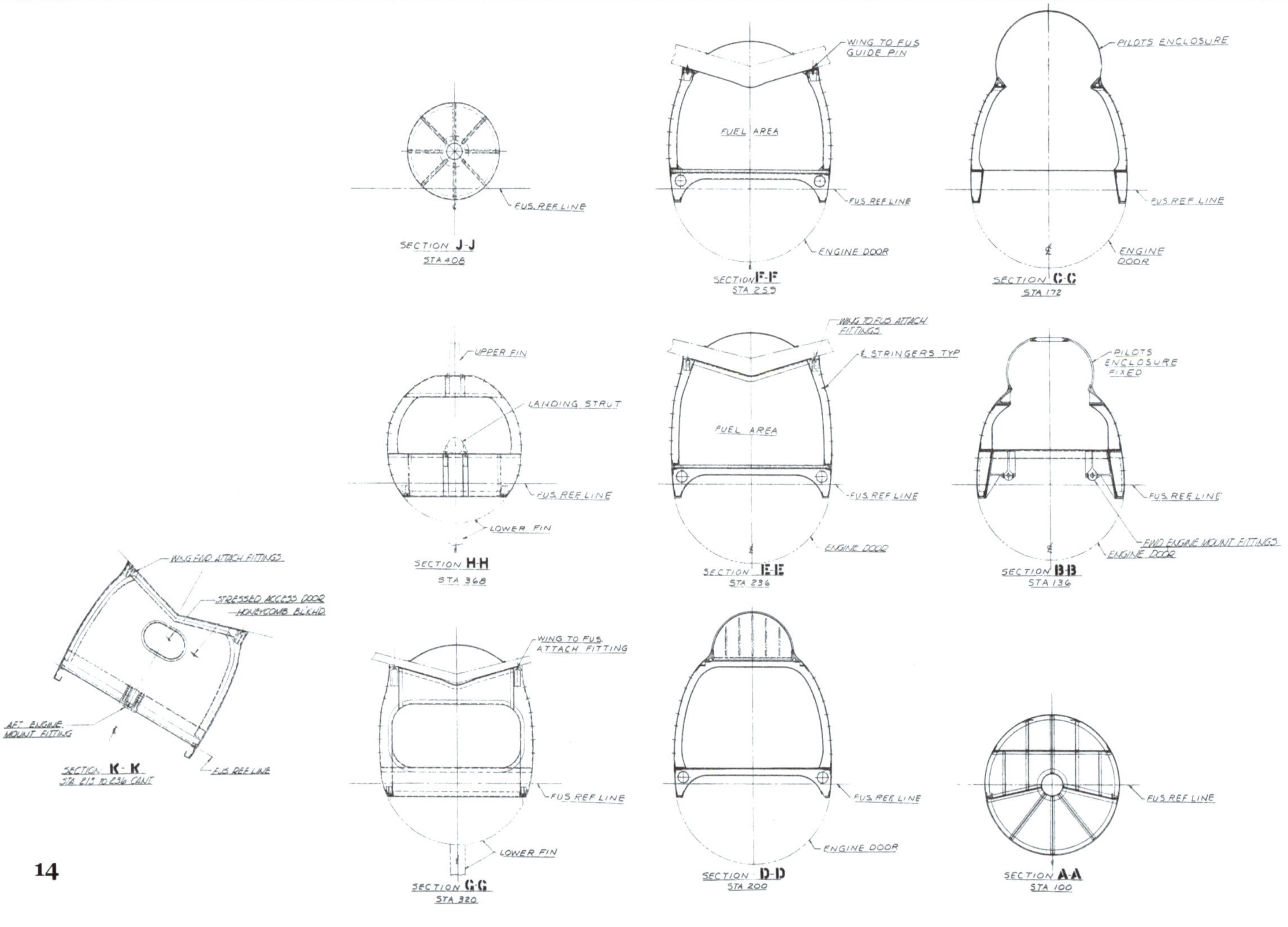

N-63 INBOARD PROFILE

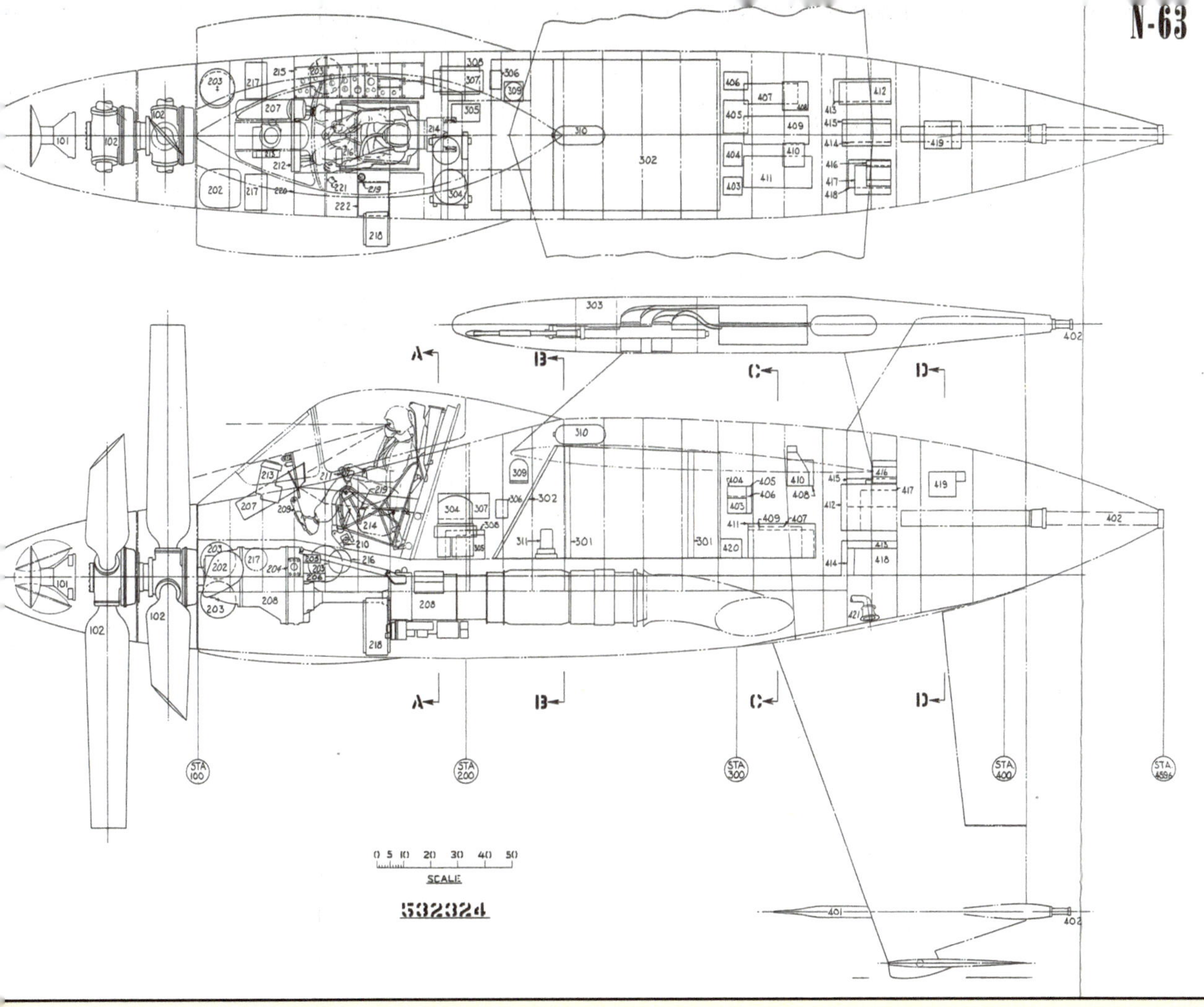

101	APG-RADAR SCREEN
102	PROPELLER 15.5 FT. DIA.
201	OIL TANK
202	OIL TANK
203	ENGINE FIRE EXTINGUISHER
204	ENGINE MOUNT
205	GENERATOR
206	STARTER
207	APG RADAR SCOPE
208	ENGINE ALLISON T40-A-8
209	RUDDER PEDALS
210	CONTROL STICK
211	THROTTLES
212	INSTRUMENT PANEL
213	MK-6 GUN SIGHT
214	EJECTION SEAT
215	ELECTRICAL CONSOLE R.H. INCLUDES:
	RADAR CONTROLS
	ARC-27 CONTROLS
	APX-6 CONTROLS
	CONTROL SWITCHES
	CIRCUIT BREAKERS
216	CONTROL FORCE BELLOWS
217	HYDRAULIC RESERVOIR
218	OIL COOLER
219	RELIEF TUBE
220	PILOT'S CONSOLE L.H. INCLUDES:
	MK-6 GUN SIGHT CONTROLS
221	OXYGEN REGULATOR
222	EMERGENCY EXIT LADDER
301	FUEL QUANTITY TRANSMITTER
302	FUEL TANK
303	ARMAMENT INCLUDES:
	MK 12 Mod 0 20 m.m. GUNS
	MK 7 FEEDERS
	GUN HEATERS
	AMMUNITION BOXES
	FEED CHUTES
	AIR CYLINDERS
304	MODULATOR & RECIEVER
305	GUN SIGHT AMPLIFIER
306	ROLL SERVO
307	APN-22 ALTITUDE TRANS. & REC.
308	AUTO-PILOT AMPLIFIER
309	VERTICAL GYRO
310	OXYGEN CYLINDER (514 cu. in.)
311	FUEL PUMP
401	PITOT TUBE
402	LANDING STRUTS
403	ARC-27 CONTROL BOX
404	AF AMPLIFIER
405	LOW VOLTAGE POWER SUPPLY
406	POWER SUPPLY
407	NAVIGATION RECEIVER
408	COMPUTER POWER SUPPLY
409	CONTROL AMPLIFIER
410	TERMINAL BOX
411	ARC-27 TRANSMITTER & RECIEVER
412	COMPUTER
413	2500 VA INVERTER
414	AMPLIFIER POWER SUPPLY
415	INDICATOR
416	P66 POWER SUPPLY
417	APX-6
418	SYNCHRONIZER
419	BATTERY
420	FUEL SUMP & PUMP
421	PRESSURE FILLER VALVE

FUSELAGE STRUCTURE

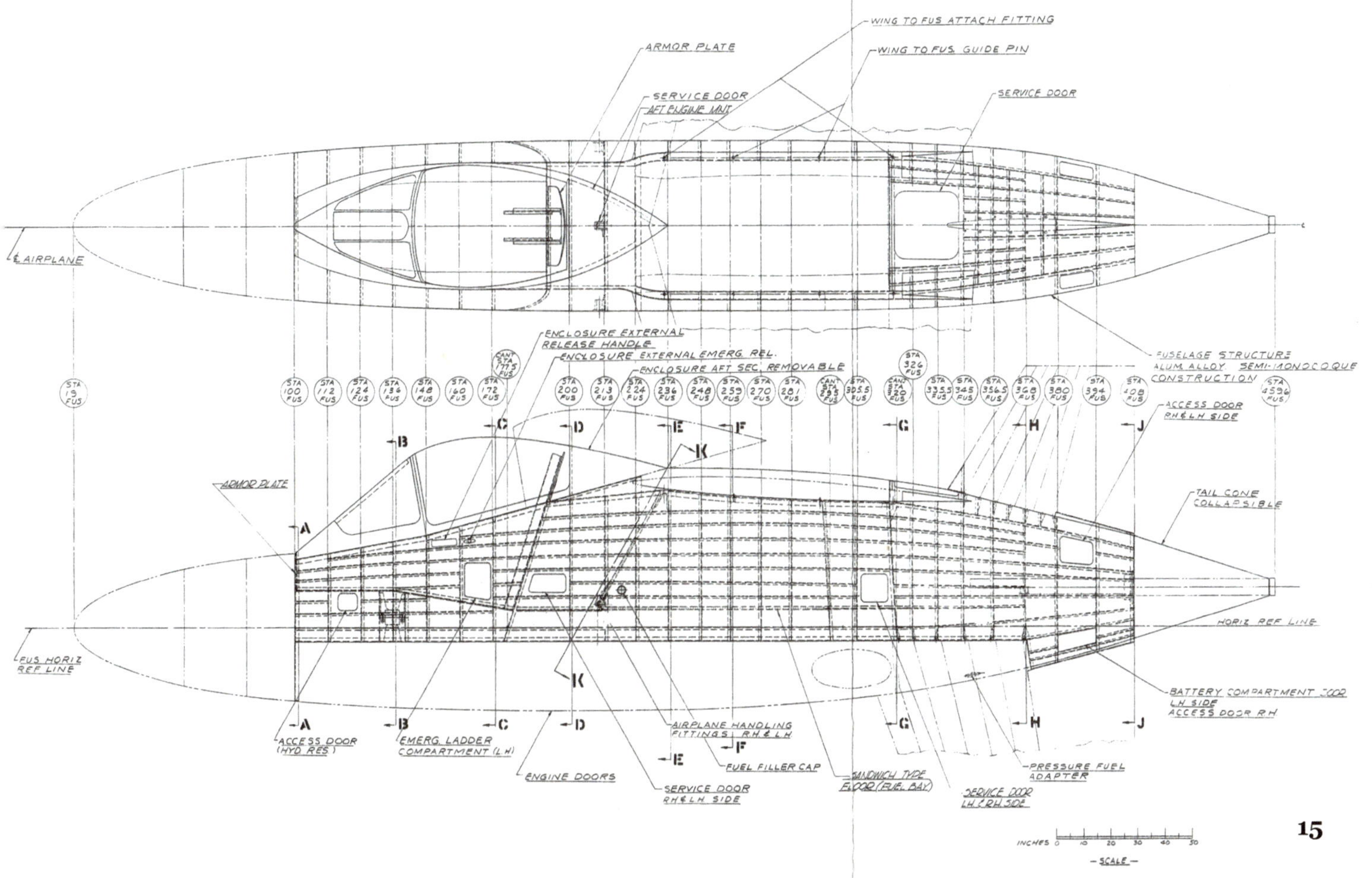

6) Schematic of the convoy fighter's empennage structure, which featured a large ventral T-tail as well as a small dorsal tail. The horizontal tail was positioned to avoid the wing wake and propeller slipstream.

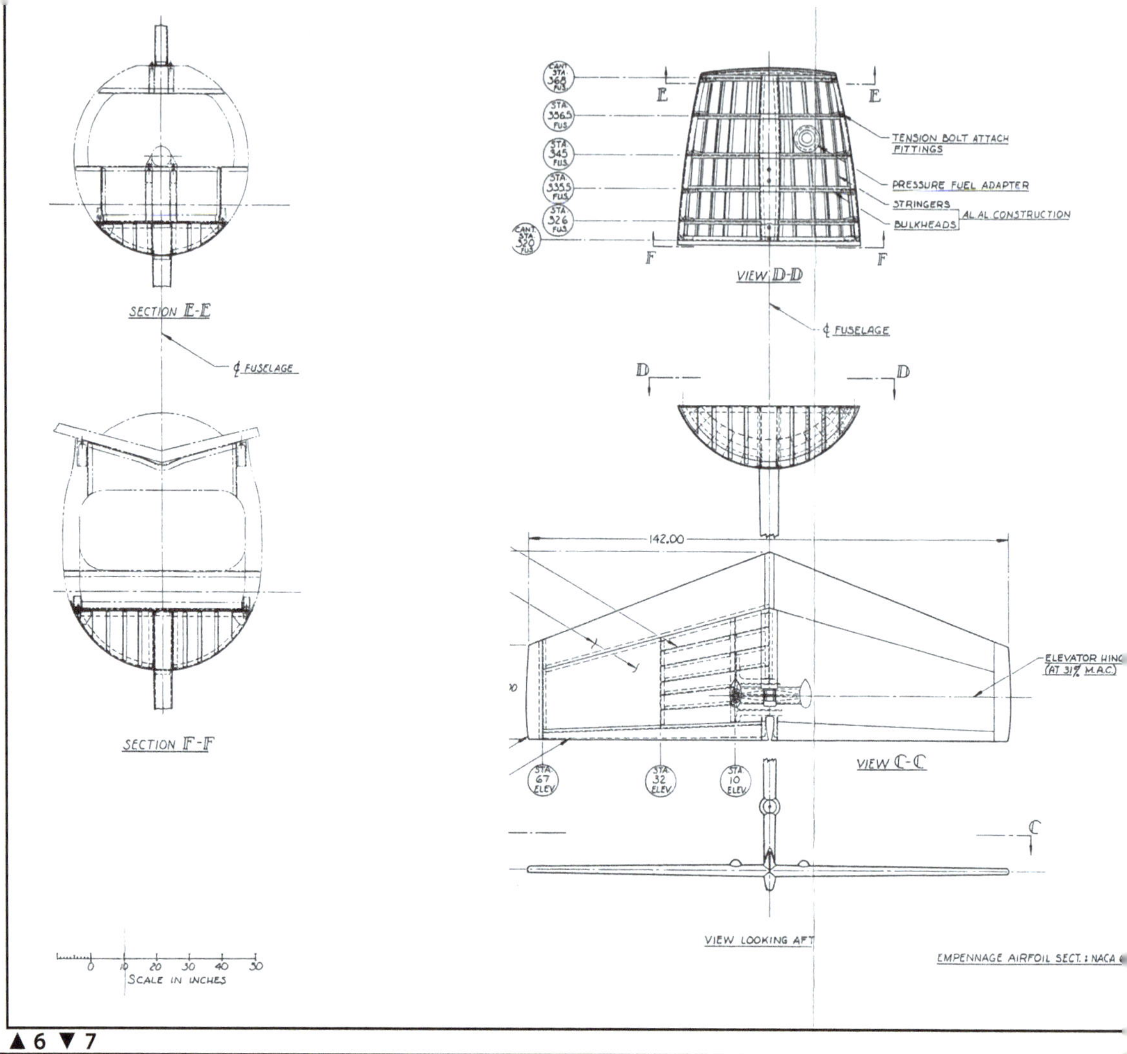

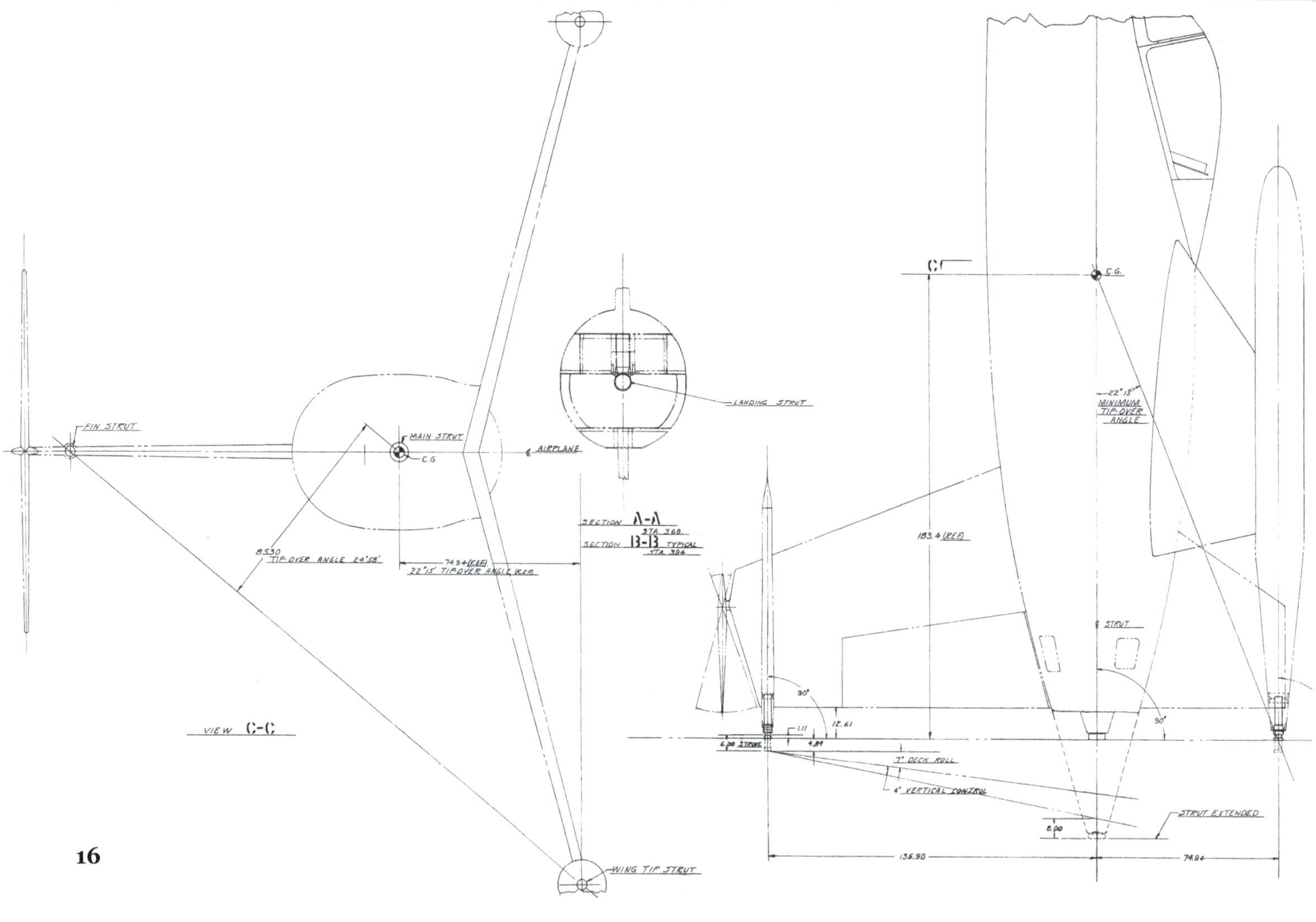

EMPENNAGE STRUCTURE

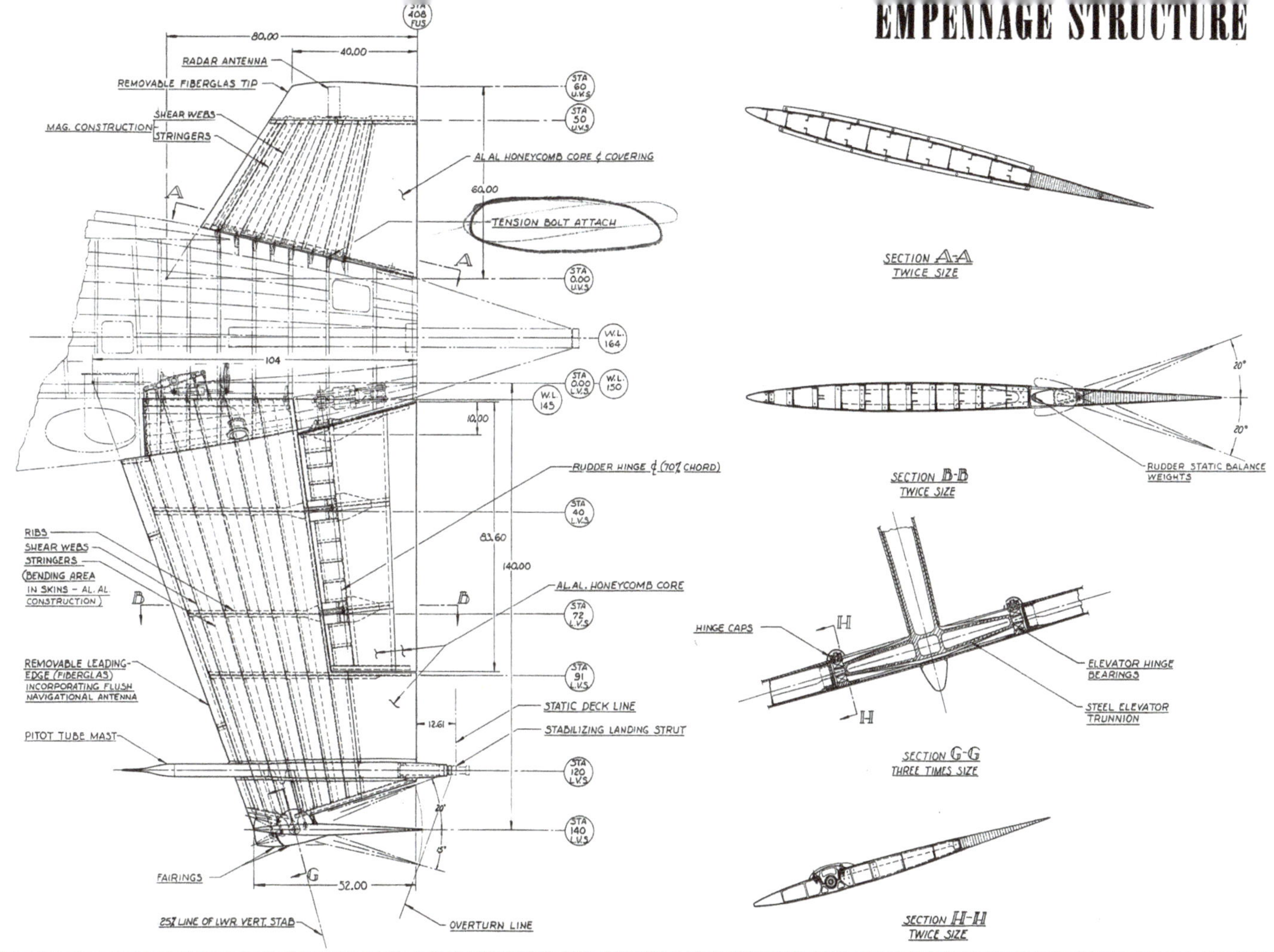

LANDING GEAR

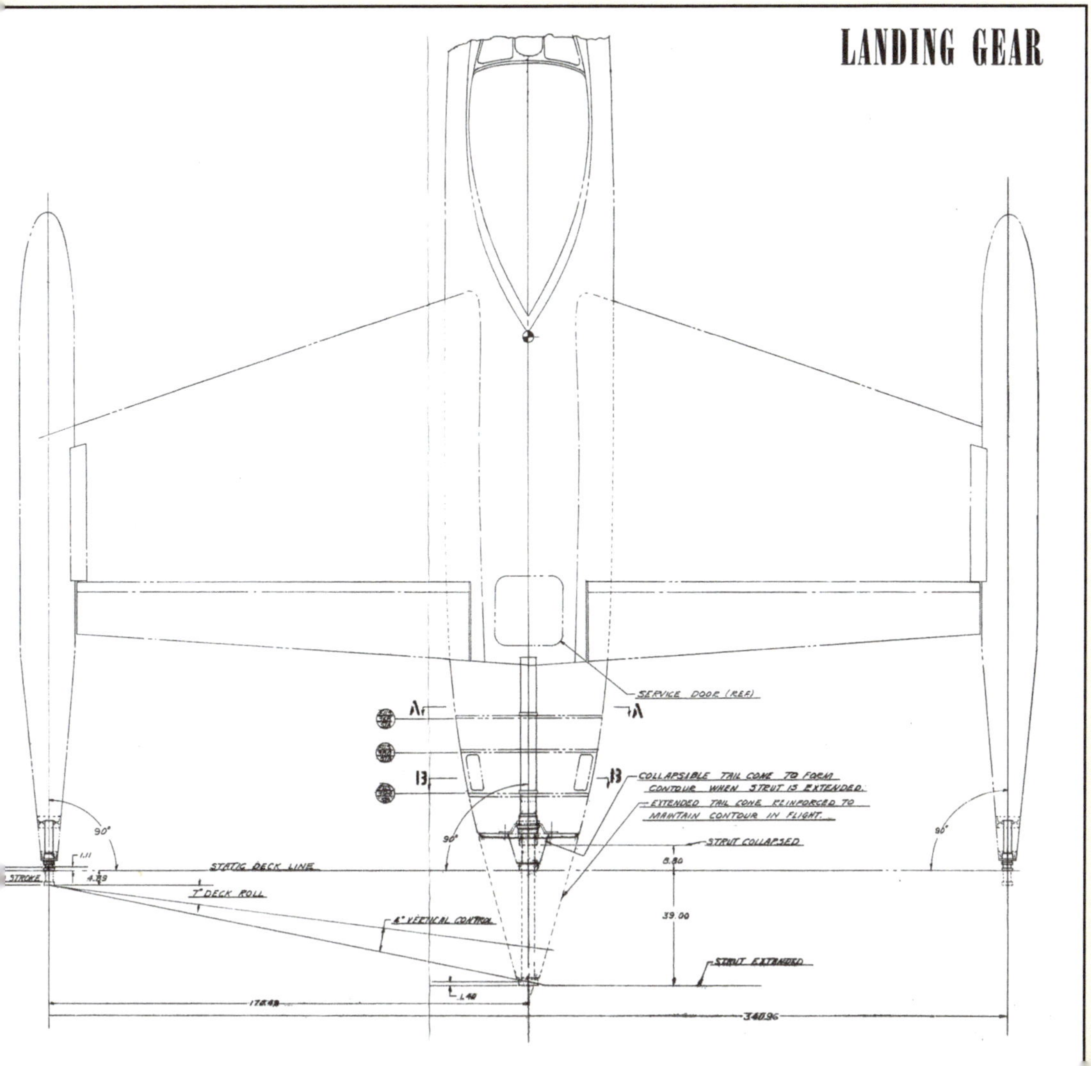

7) The N-63's landing gear featured small shock absorbers at the wing tips and vertical stabilizer tip, as well as a robust landing strut in the tail cone, which was made of a flexible nonmetallic material that collapsed upon landing.

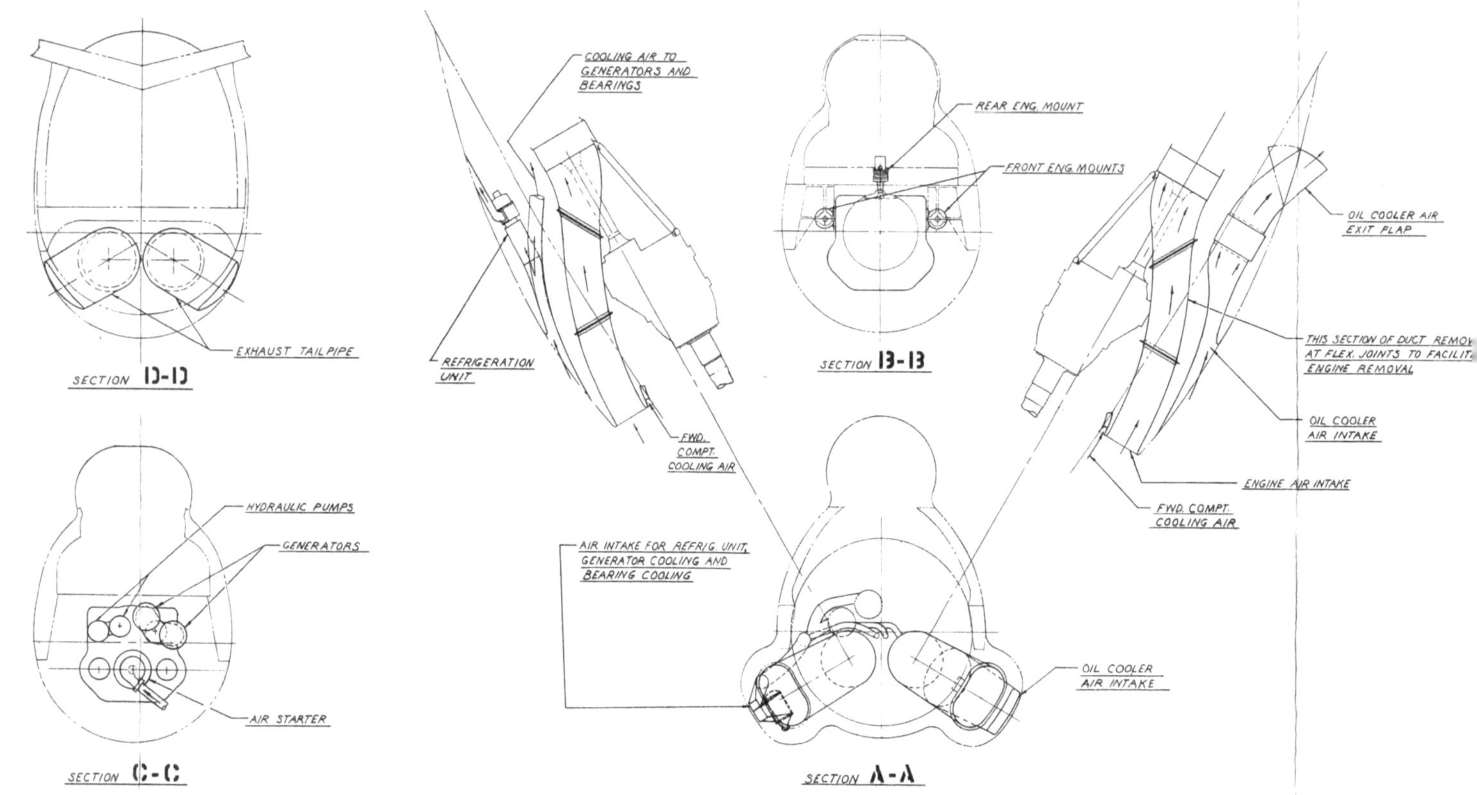

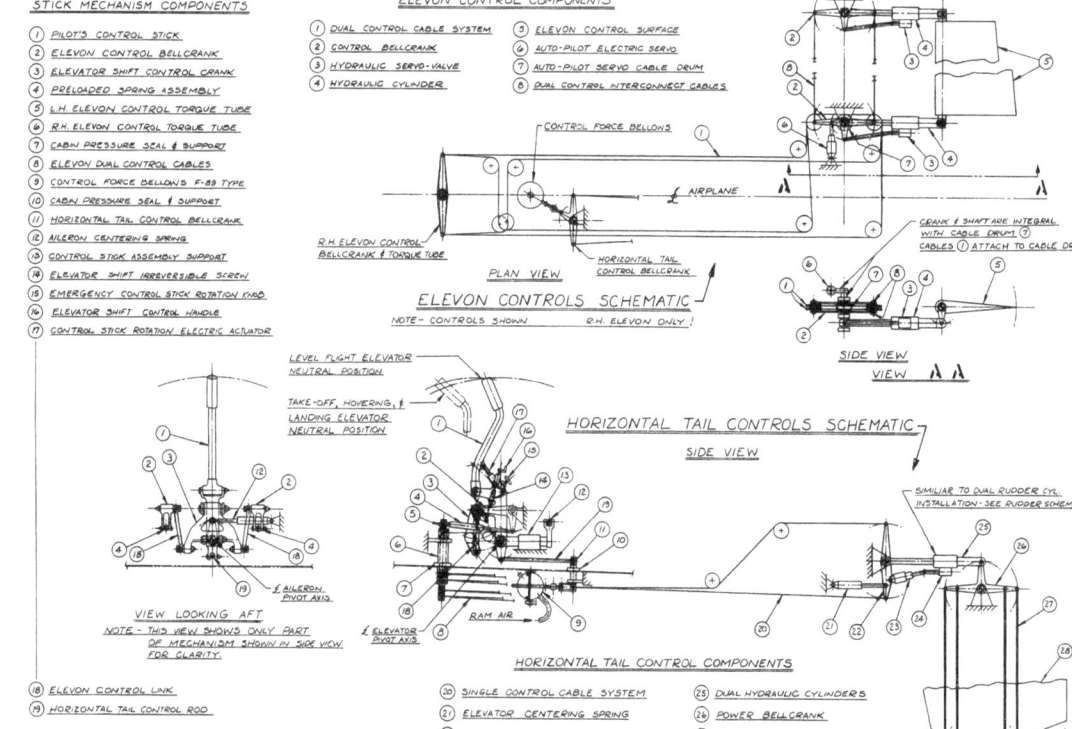

ELEVON & HORIZONTAL CONTROLS OPERATION

SUBJECT POWER CONTROL SYSTEMS OPERATE IDENTICAL TO RUDDER SYSTEM. SEE "RUDDER CONTROLS OPERATION".

DESIGN NOTES - GENERAL

I HYDRAULIC SYSTEMS - SEE RUDDER CONTROLS DESIGN NOTE #1

II CONTROL STICK MECHANISM

A. HORIZONTAL TAIL CONTROLS.
THIS CONTROL OPERATES AS A CONVENTIONAL ELEVATOR CONTROL SYSTEM. PILOT'S CONTROL STICK ① ROTATES ABOUT ELEVATOR PIVOT AXIS SHOWN, TRANSMITS MOTION THROUGH CONTROL ROD ⑲, OPERATES CONTROL BELLCRANK ⑪, ROTATING THROUGH CABIN PRESSURE SEAL ⑩, MOVES CONTROL CABLE SYSTEM.

B. ELEVON CONTROLS
 1 - HOVERING, TAKE-OFF, & LANDING CONDITIONS -
 ELEVATOR AND AILERON MOTIONS ARE COMBINED PROVIDING ELEVON CONTROL FOR THESE FLIGHT CONDITIONS. CRANK ③ IS ROTATED TO "FULL ELEVATOR" POSITION SHOWN, BY PILOT OPERATION OF CONTROL HANDLE ⑯, OPERATES IRREVERSIBLE SCREW ⑭, LOCKS CRANK ③ RELATIVE TO PILOT'S CONTROL STICK ①. THUS PILOT OPERATION OF CONTROL STICK IN ELEVATOR & AILERON DIRECTIONS TRANSMITS MOTION TO LINK ⑱ AT ITS CONNECTION TO CRANK ③, ROTATES BELLCRANK'S ②, MOVES PRELOADED SPRING ASSEMBLIES ④, ROTATES L.H. ELEVON & R.H. ELEVON TORQUE TUBES ⑤⑥, WHICH DRIVES ELEVON CONTROL CABLES ⑧.

 2 - LEVEL FLIGHT CONDITION -
 ELEVATOR CONTROL IS ELIMINATED FOR THIS FLIGHT CONDITION. THUS ELEVONS FUNCTION AS AILERONS ONLY. TO ELIMINATE ELEVATOR MOTION FROM THE ELEVONS, THE PILOT OPERATES CONTROL HANDLE ⑯ WHICH ROTATES CRANK ③ FROM THE "FULL ELEVATOR" SHOWN UNTIL ITS LOWER END ATTACHMENT TO LINK ⑱ COINCIDES WITH ELEVATOR PIVOT AXIS. IN THIS "ZERO ELEVATOR" POSITION, ELEVATOR MOTION OF THE CONTROL STICK WILL NOT TRANSMIT MOTION TO THE ELEVON CONTROL SYSTEM. AILERON CONTROL IS NOT AFFECTED BY THIS CHANGE IN THE ELEVATOR CONTROL SYSTEM. BECAUSE THE PILOT'S MECHANICAL ADVANTAGE OVER THE CONTROL SYSTEM IS INFINITE AT THE "ZERO ELEVATOR" POSITION, PRELOADED SPRING ASSEMBLY ④ IS USED TO LIMIT THE LOAD THAT CAN BE TRANSMITTED TO THE CONTROL SYSTEM. THE PRELOAD IS HIGH ENOUGH THAT THE SPRING WILL NOT COMPRESS DURING NORMAL OPERATING CONDITIONS.

C - CONTROL FORCE PRODUCERS
 1 - ELEVATOR -
 CONTROL FORCES ARE PRODUCED BY ELEVATOR CENTERING SPRING ㉑ AT HORIZONTAL TAIL SERVO-VALVE MECHANISM, AND F-89 TYPE AERODYNAMIC FORCE BELLOWS ⑨ AT HORIZONTAL TAIL CONTROL BELLCRANK ⑪. STICK FORCES WILL BE APPROXIMATELY 7 LBS. PER 'g' FOR AS GREAT A PART OF THE FLIGHT RANGE AS POSSIBLE. CENTERING SPRING ㉑ WILL CENTER THE HORIZONTAL TAIL SHOULD THE CONTROL CABLE SYSTEM BE SEVERED.

 2 - AILERON -
 CONTROL FORCES ARE PRODUCED BY AILERON CENTERING SPRING ⑫. FORCES WILL VARY DIRECTLY WITH AILERON STICK POSITION, BEING ZERO AT NEUTRAL AND 15 LBS. AT FULL AILERON POSITIONS.

III ELEVATOR TRIM, AILERON TRIM & AILERON DROOP
PILOT OPERATION OF TRIM CONTROL SWITCHES ACTUATES ELEVATOR AUTO-PILOT SERVO ④, HORIZONTAL TAIL ELEVATOR TRIM ACTUATOR ㉓. AILERON DROOP OF 6° MAX. WILL BE AUTOMATICALLY CONTROLLED BY AN ELECTRICAL SIGNAL FROM AN ACCELEROMETER MEASURING AIRPLANE NORMAL ACCELERATION, ACTUATES ELEVON AUTO-PILOT SERVO.

IV ELEVON AUTO-PILOT & HORIZONTAL TAIL ELEVATOR TRIM OPERATION
SUBJECT SERVOS ARE IN MECHANICAL SERIES WITH ELEVON & HORIZONTAL CONTROL SYSTEMS. SERVO TRAVEL IS INDEPENDENT OF CONTROL POSITION & VISA VERSA. WHEN CONTROL SYSTEM TRAVEL IS IN THE SAME DIRECTION AS SERVO TRAVEL, THE RESULTANT CONTROL SURFACE DISPLACEMENT WILL BE THE SUM OF THE TWO. WHEN THE TRAVELS ARE IN OPPOSITE DIRECTIONS, THE RESULTANT CONTROL SURFACE DISPLACEMENT WILL BE DIFFERENCE BETWEEN THEM & IN THE DIRECTION OF THE GREATER OF THE TWO.

STICK MECHANISM COMPONENTS

① PILOT'S CONTROL STICK
② ELEVON CONTROL BELLCRANK
③ ELEVATOR SHIFT CONTROL CRANK
④ PRELOADED SPRING ASSEMBLY
⑤ L.H. ELEVON CONTROL TORQUE TUBE
⑥ R.H. ELEVON CONTROL TORQUE TUBE
⑦ CABIN PRESSURE SEAL & SUPPORT
⑧ ELEVON DUAL CONTROL CABLES
⑨ CONTROL FORCE BELLOWS F-89 TYPE
⑩ CABIN PRESSURE SEAL & SUPPORT
⑪ HORIZONTAL TAIL CONTROL BELLCRANK
⑫ AILERON CENTERING SPRING
⑬ CONTROL STICK ASSEMBLY SUPPORT
⑭ ELEVATOR SHIFT IRREVERSIBLE SCREW
⑮ EMERGENCY CONTROL STICK ROTATION KNOB
⑯ ELEVATOR SHIFT CONTROL HANDLE
⑰ CONTROL STICK ROTATION ELECTRIC ACTUATOR
⑱ ELEVON CONTROL LINK
⑲ HORIZONTAL TAIL CONTROL ROD

ELEVON CONTROL COMPONENTS

① DUAL CONTROL CABLE SYSTEM
② CONTROL BELLCRANK
③ HYDRAULIC SERVO-VALVE
④ HYDRAULIC CYLINDER
⑤ ELEVON CONTROL SURFACE
⑥ AUTO-PILOT ELECTRIC SERVO
⑦ AUTO-PILOT SERVO CABLE DRUM
⑧ DUAL CONTROL INTERCONNECT CABLES

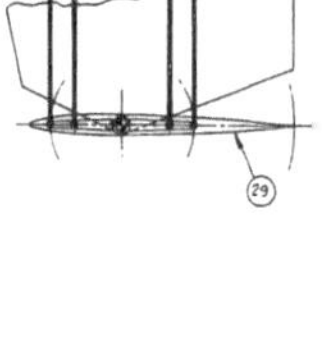

HORIZONTAL TAIL CONTROL COMPONENTS

⑳ SINGLE CONTROL CABLE SYSTEM
㉑ ELEVATOR CENTERING SPRING
㉒ CONTROL BELLCRANK
㉓ ELEVATOR TRIM ELECTRIC ACTUATOR
㉔ DUAL HYDRAULIC SERVO-VALVES
㉕ DUAL HYDRAULIC CYLINDERS
㉖ POWER BELLCRANK
㉗ DUAL POWER TENSION RODS
㉘ RUDDER & VERTICAL STABILIZER
㉙ HORIZONTAL TAIL CONTROL SURFACE

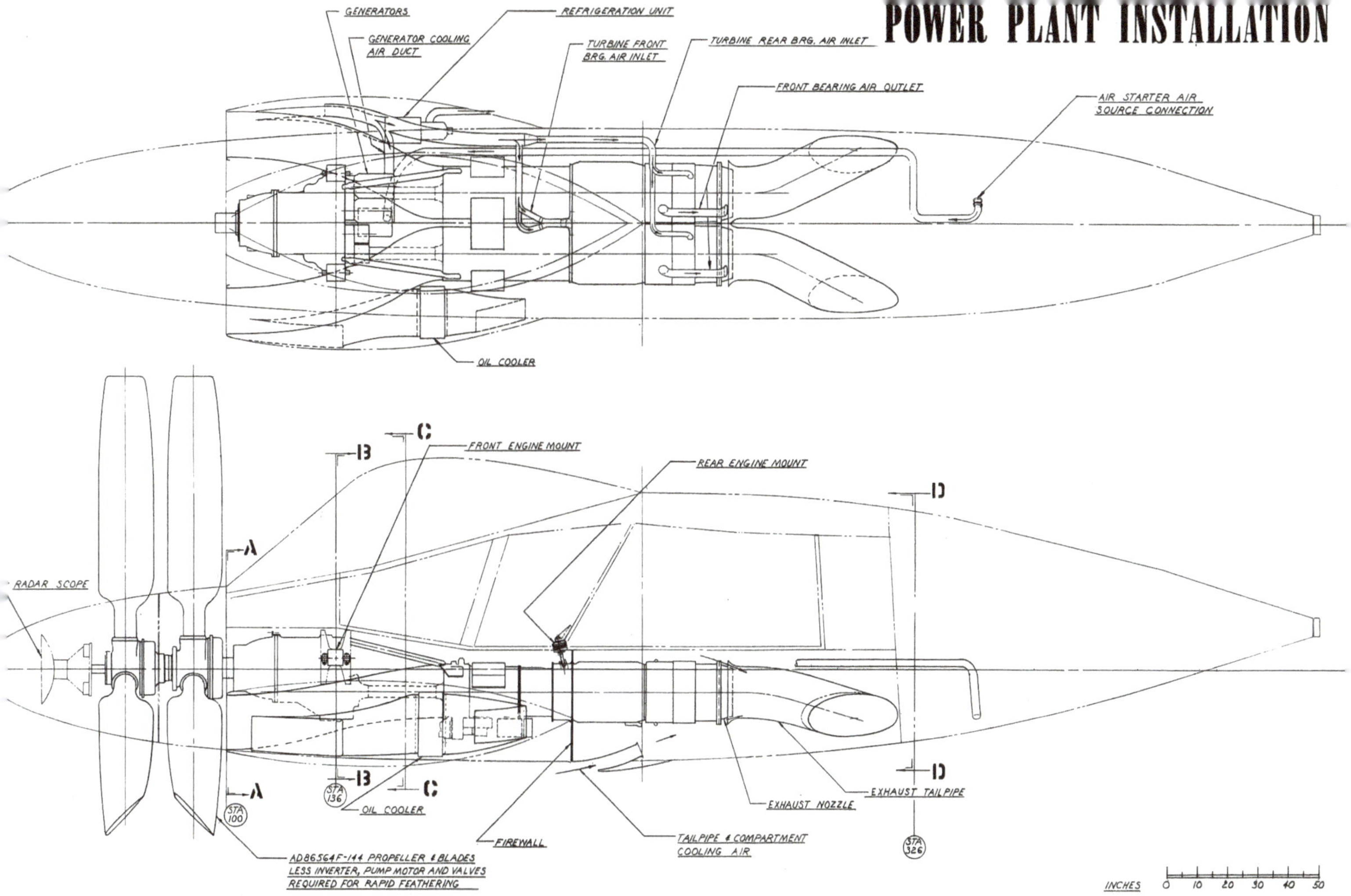

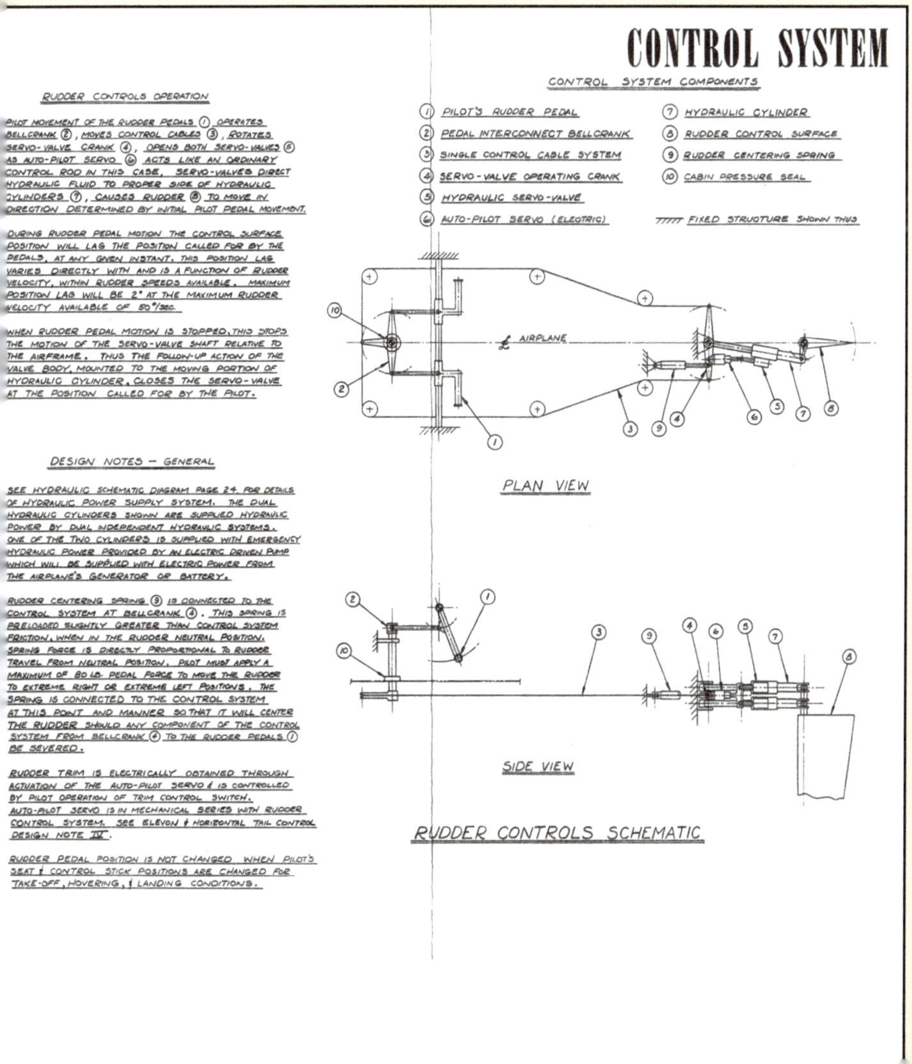

POWER PLANT INSTALLATION

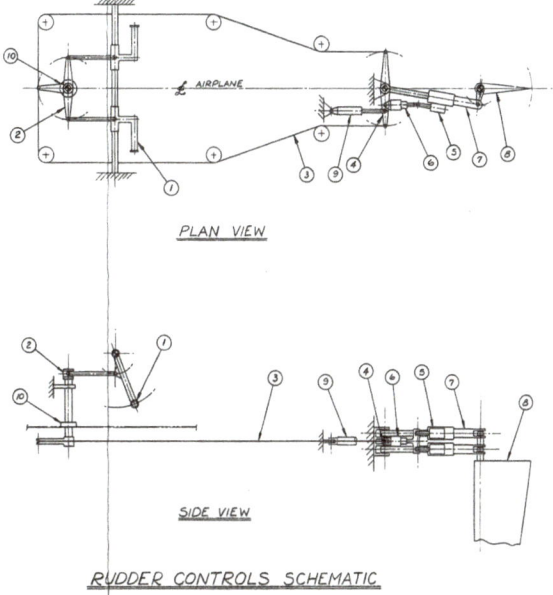

8) Blueprint of the N-63's power plant installation, which consisted of an Allison XT-40-A-8 turboprop engine driving an Aeroproducts 15.5 ft six-blade dual-rotation propeller.

9) Schematic of the Northrop convoy fighter's fully powered control system. The elevons and rudder provided control during hovering, transition, and takeoff and landing. The elevons also provided roll and pitch and control, while the rudder contributed to yaw control.

10) The N-63 was armed with four 20 mm aircraft guns and 600 rounds of ammunition mounted in wing tip pods.

11) Diagram of the convoy fighter's external antenna locations, the largest of which was the AN/APG-37 gun laying radar mounted in the nose.

12) The N-63's fuel system featured a single fuselage tank and sump with a total usable capacity of 552 gallons.

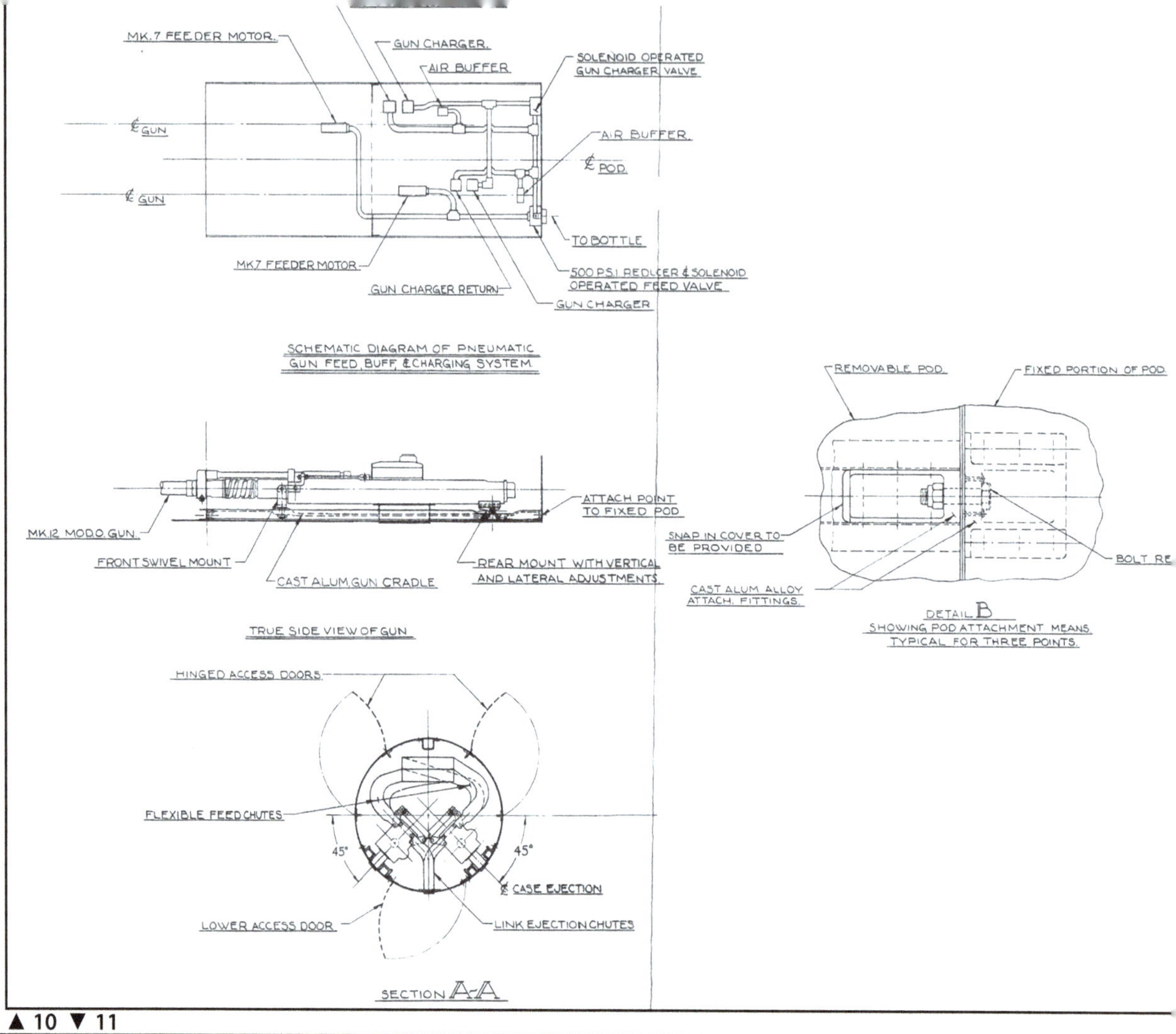

▲ 10 ▼ 11

EXTERNAL ANTENNA LOCATION

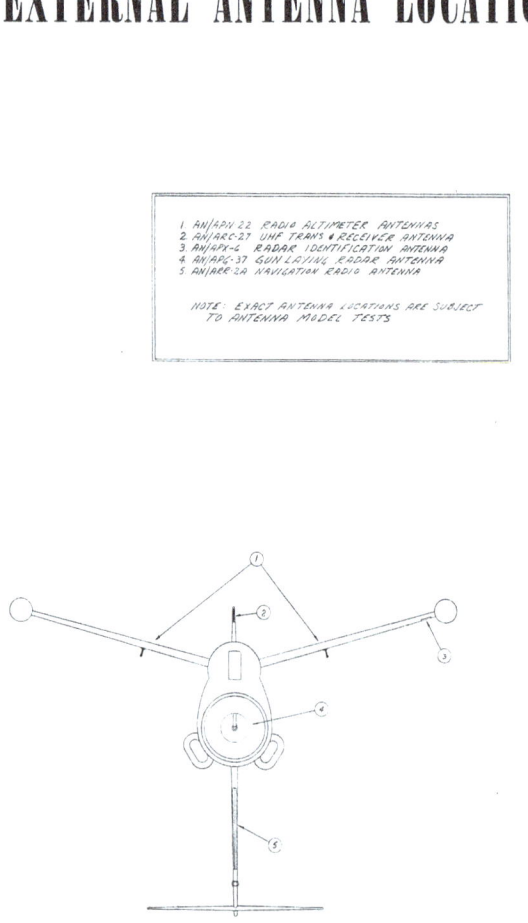
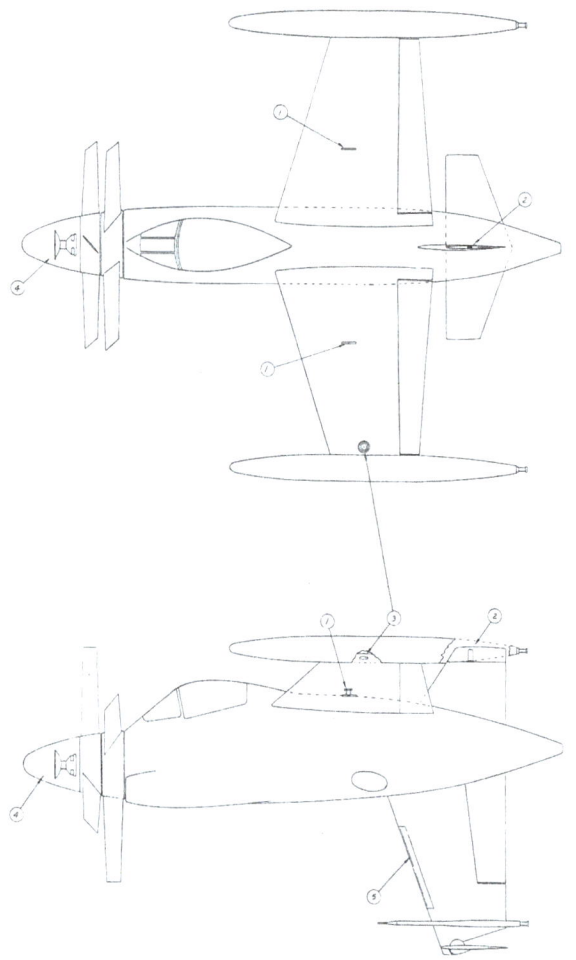

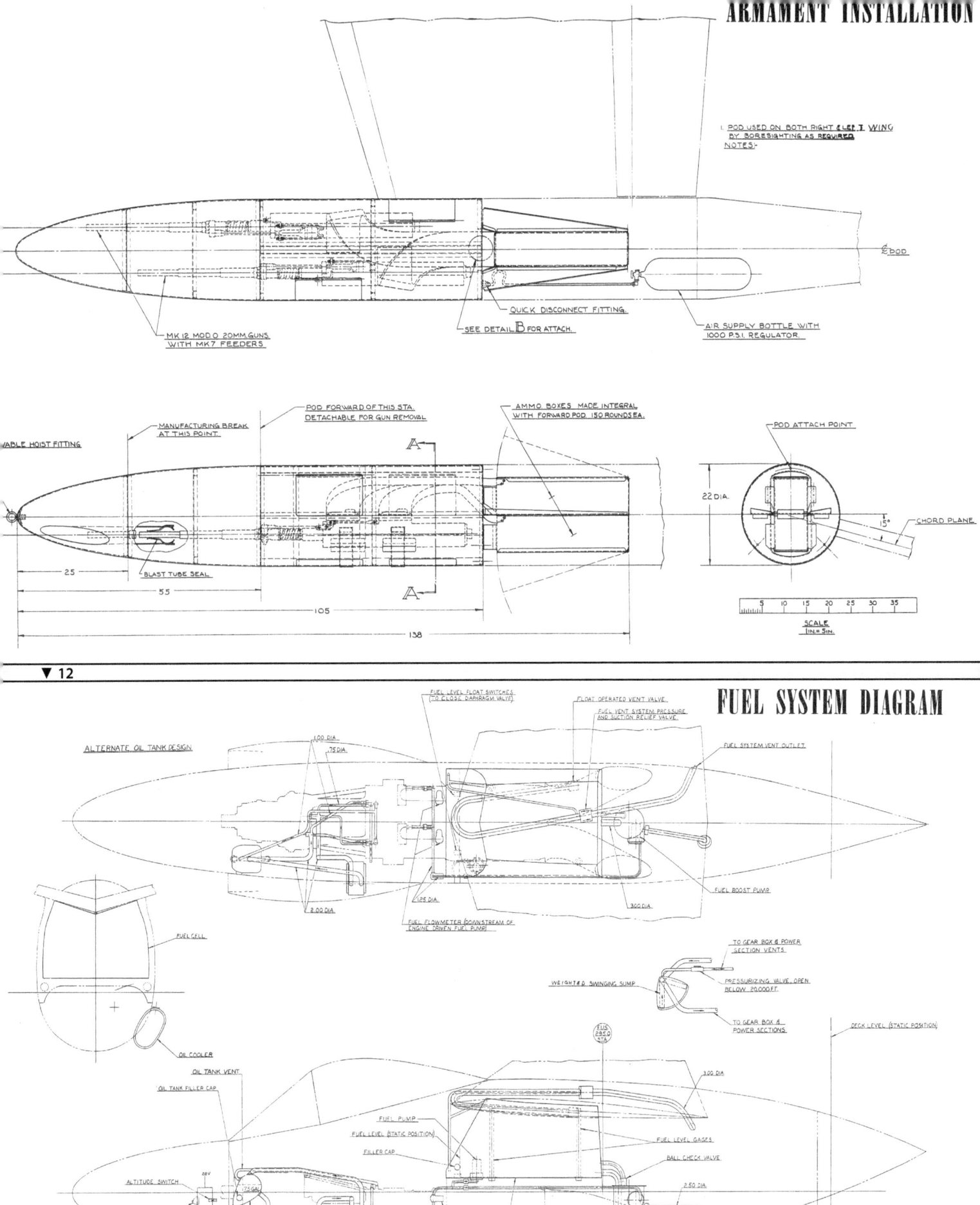

▲ 13 ▼ 14

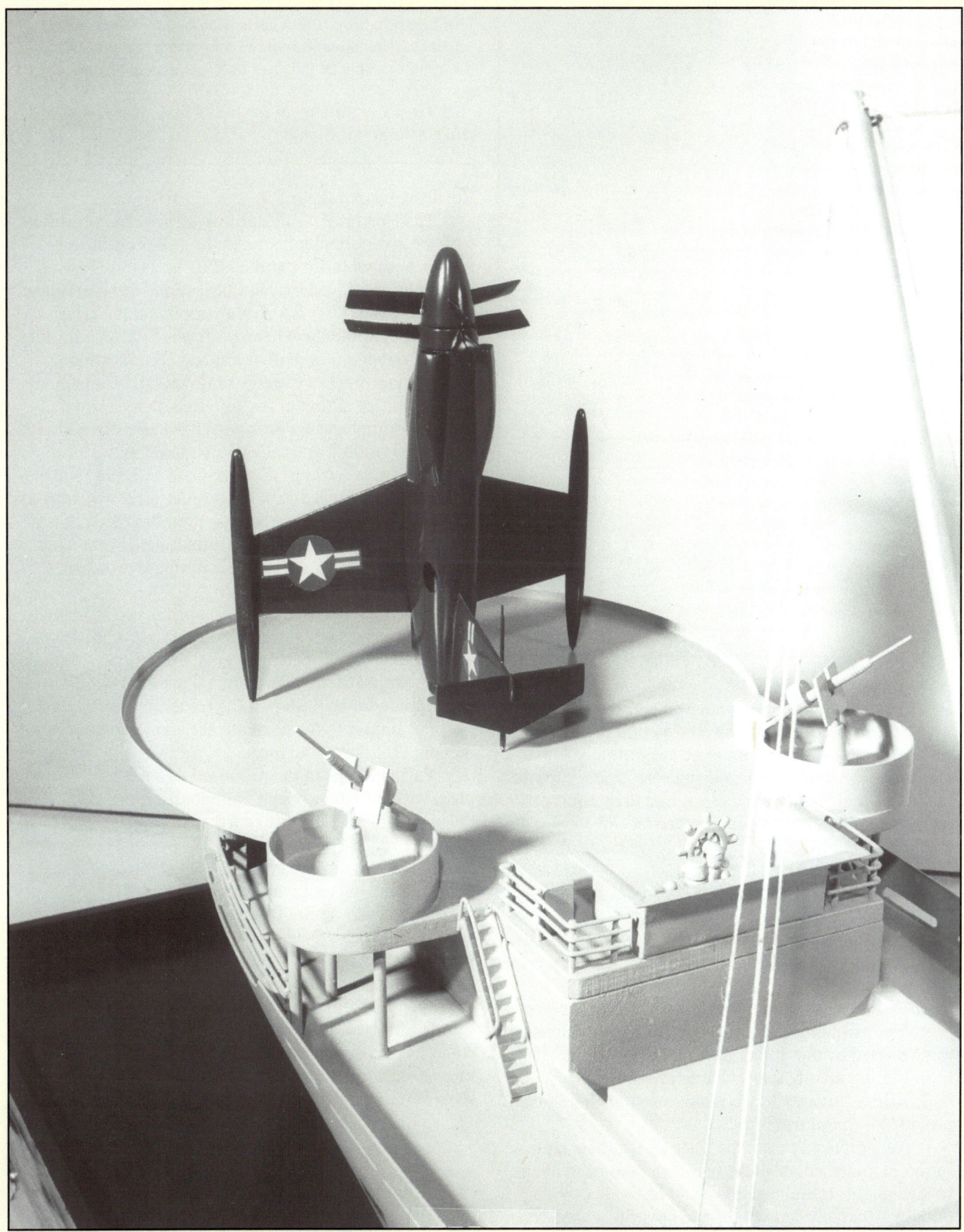

▲ 15

13-15) Northrop was one of the few contractors to construct an elaborate desktop model of their convoy fighter proposal, along with a section of the merchant vessel it would have operated from. The ship required a minimum of modification to operate the N-63, which did not need a hoisting apparatus since it was in the takeoff attitude at all times.

Northrop N-63A

16) The Northrop N-63A scale prototype could be fitted either with a conventional tail for normal takeoff and landing or a special tailsitter unit for vertical testing.

17) Artist's impression of the N-63A taking off vertically from a desert location.

Northrop design of the experimental prototype vertically-rising airplane involved two primary considerations. First, it had to be a flying aerodynamic model of the full-scale fighter. Second, it had to be equipped with an auxiliary landing gear to permit conventional takeoff and landing for exploration of unconventional transition and hovering flight characteristics at altitudes where takeoff and landing considerations would not be involved.

Extensive studies of the full-scale N-63 convoy fighter resulted in an optimum configuration for a vertically-rising airplane. Its design was in no way compromised by conventional landing requirements of the prototype airplane. The primary prototype requirement was satisfied by development of a design most nearly representing aerodynamic characteristics of the full-scale fighter. An auxiliary landing gear was therefore provided for pilot training.

The proposed prototype design permitted exploration of intermediate steps between conventional and vertical flight. Initial takeoffs could be made conventionally to explore level flight and hovering characteristics at safe altitudes. Simple modifications of the basic configuration permitted perfection of vertical takeoff and landing techniques. Short progressive steps from conventional to vertical flight were prime features of the Northrop proposal.

The Northrop N-63A prototype airplane was fitted with a conventional tail and landing gear for initial flights. Normal takeoff and landing procedures would have been employed for familiarization with level flight characteristics, after which transition and hovering maneuvers would have been performed at safe altitudes without danger of takeoff or landing complications.

Replacement of the conventional tail by one more representative of that of the full-scale fighter and removal of the landing gear permitted investigation of vertical landing and takeoff characteristics. Initial hovering tests would have been made with the airplane tethered for control of test conditions, after which free-flight takeoff would have been accomplished. Aerodynamic characteristics of the full-scale fighter would have been investigated with this ultimate prototype configuration.

Thus the proposed Northrop prototype airplane permitted progressive transition from conventional to vertical flight. A properly designed autopilot could have been modified to provide correct flight characteristics as appropriate for each step in the transition from a simple pilot trainer to the ultimate aerodynamic model of the convoy fighter.

Various steps in the proposed program could have been eliminated at the Navy's discretion, with corresponding savings in cost. For example, since the configuration with a conventional tail and landing gear was merely a pilot trainer, it may have been desirable to eliminate the first stages of the program and commence with the tethered ultimate configuration. Sufficient pilot familiarization could have probably been achieved, with more accurate representation of full-scale aerodynamic characteristics.

ROTOTYPE CONFIGURATIONS

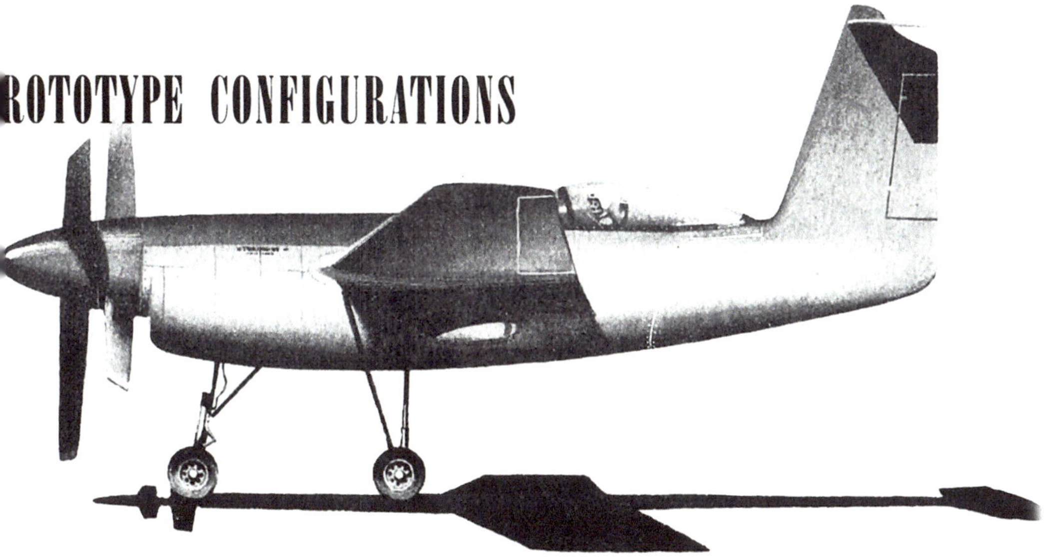

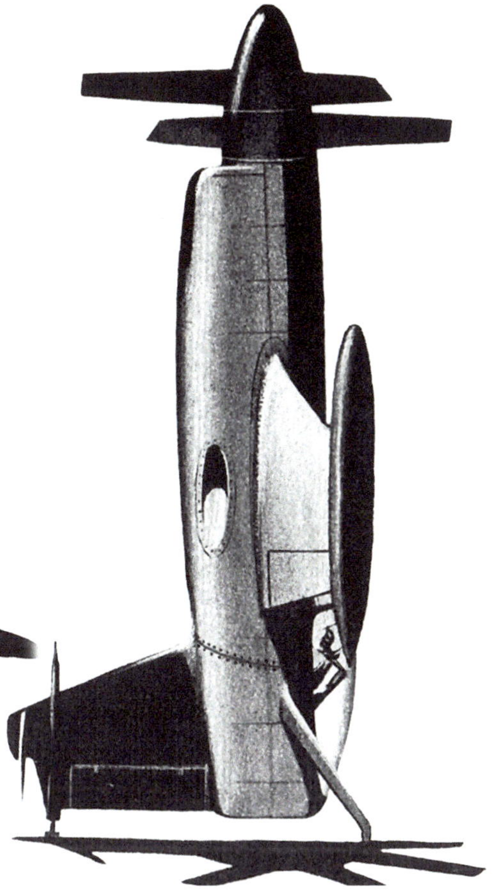

▲ 16 ▼ 17

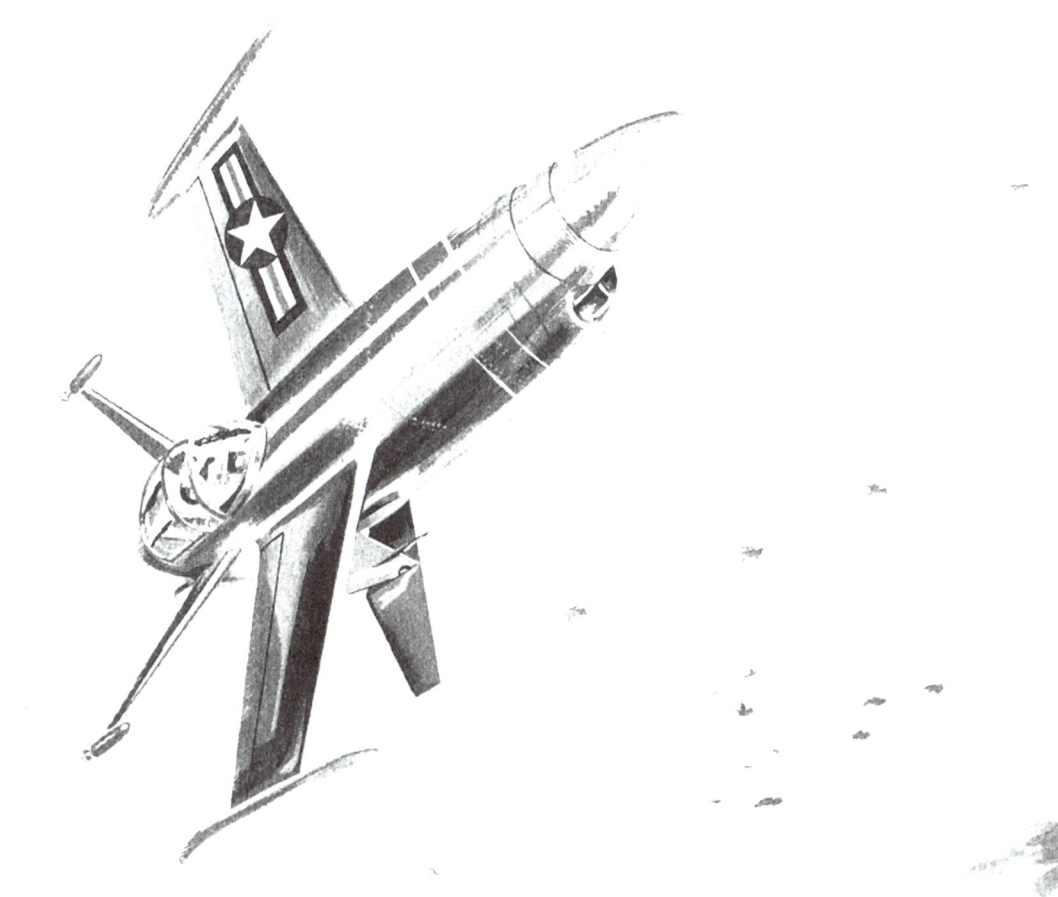

N-63A TAKE-OFF

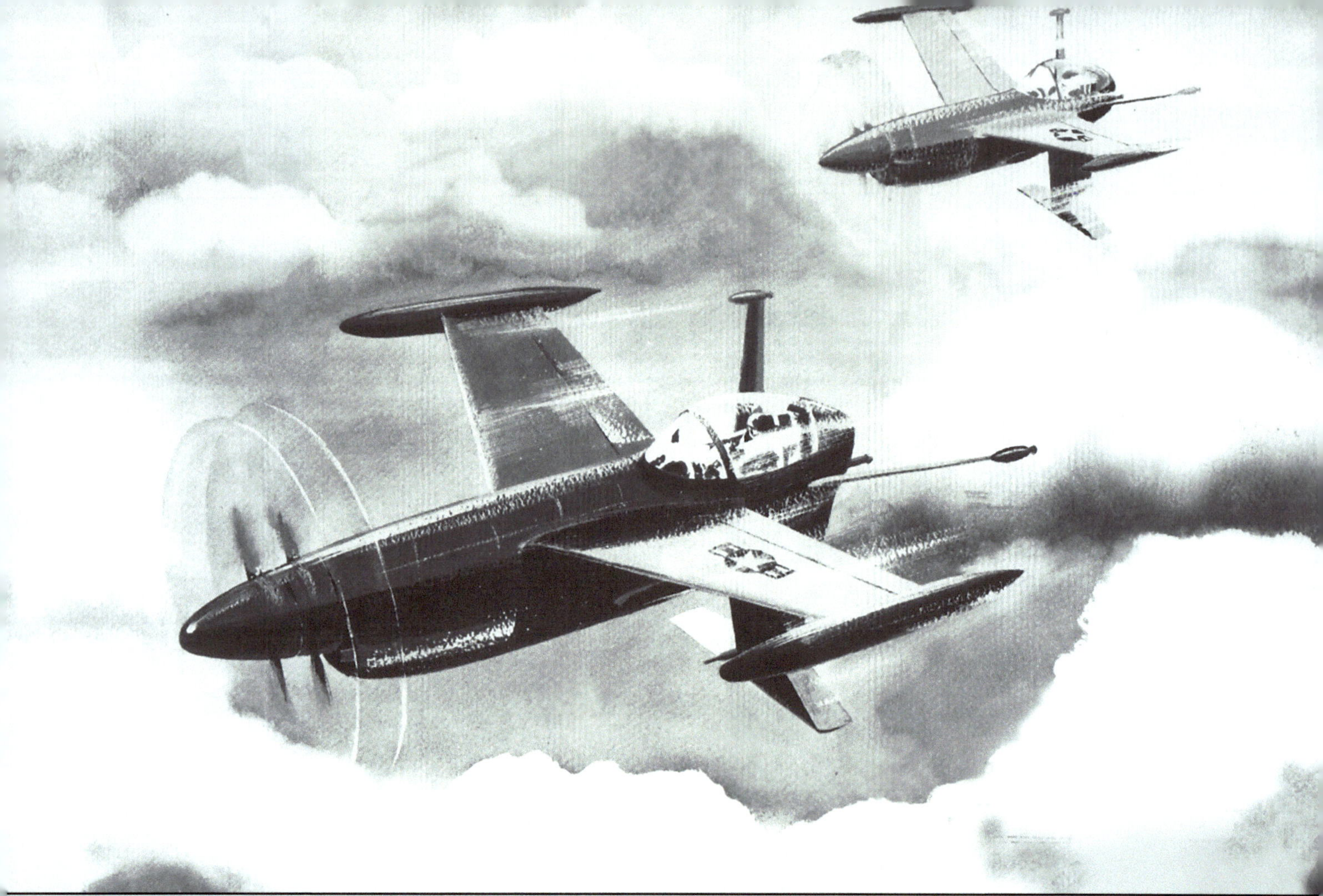

▲ 18 ▼ 19

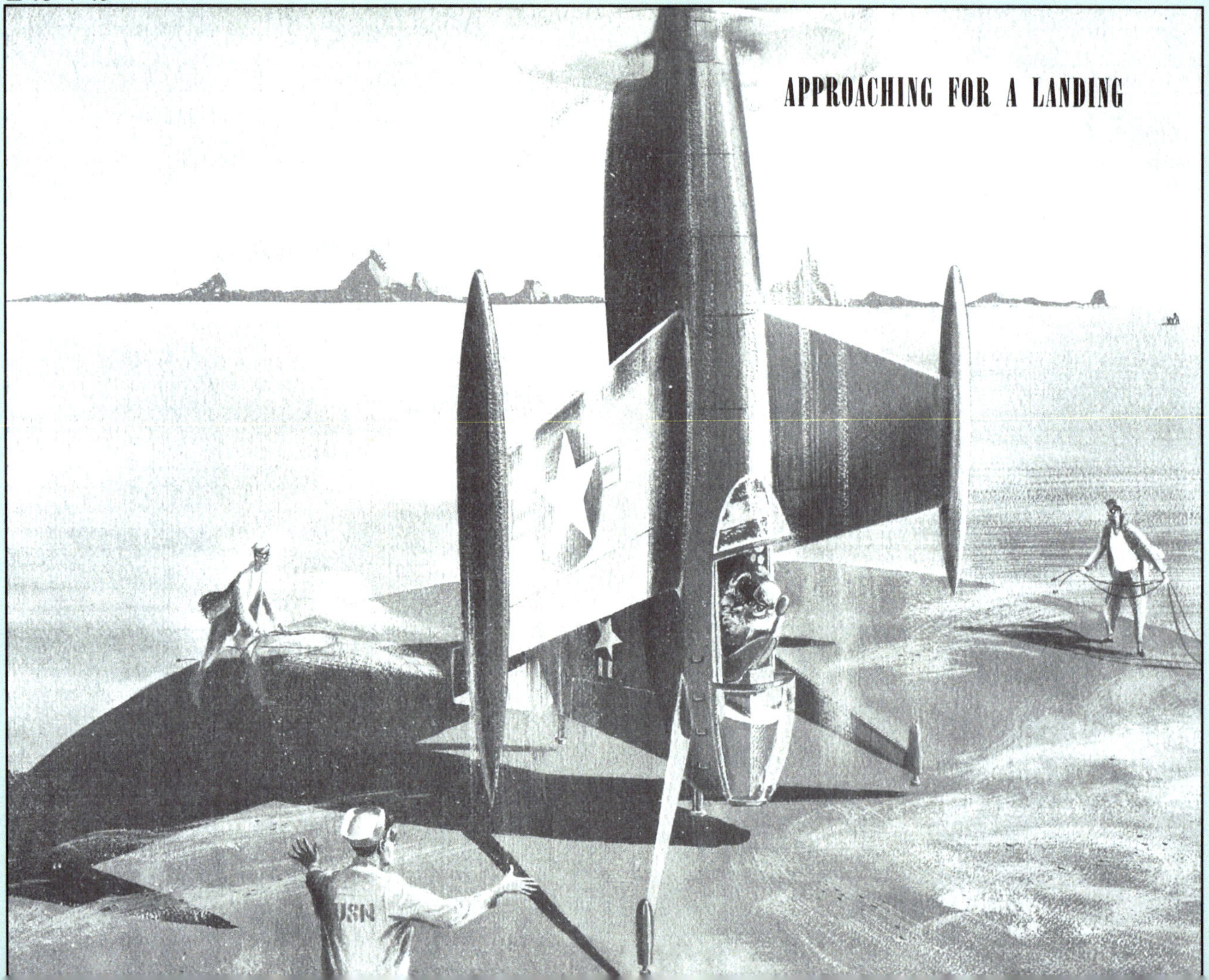

APPROACHING FOR A LANDING

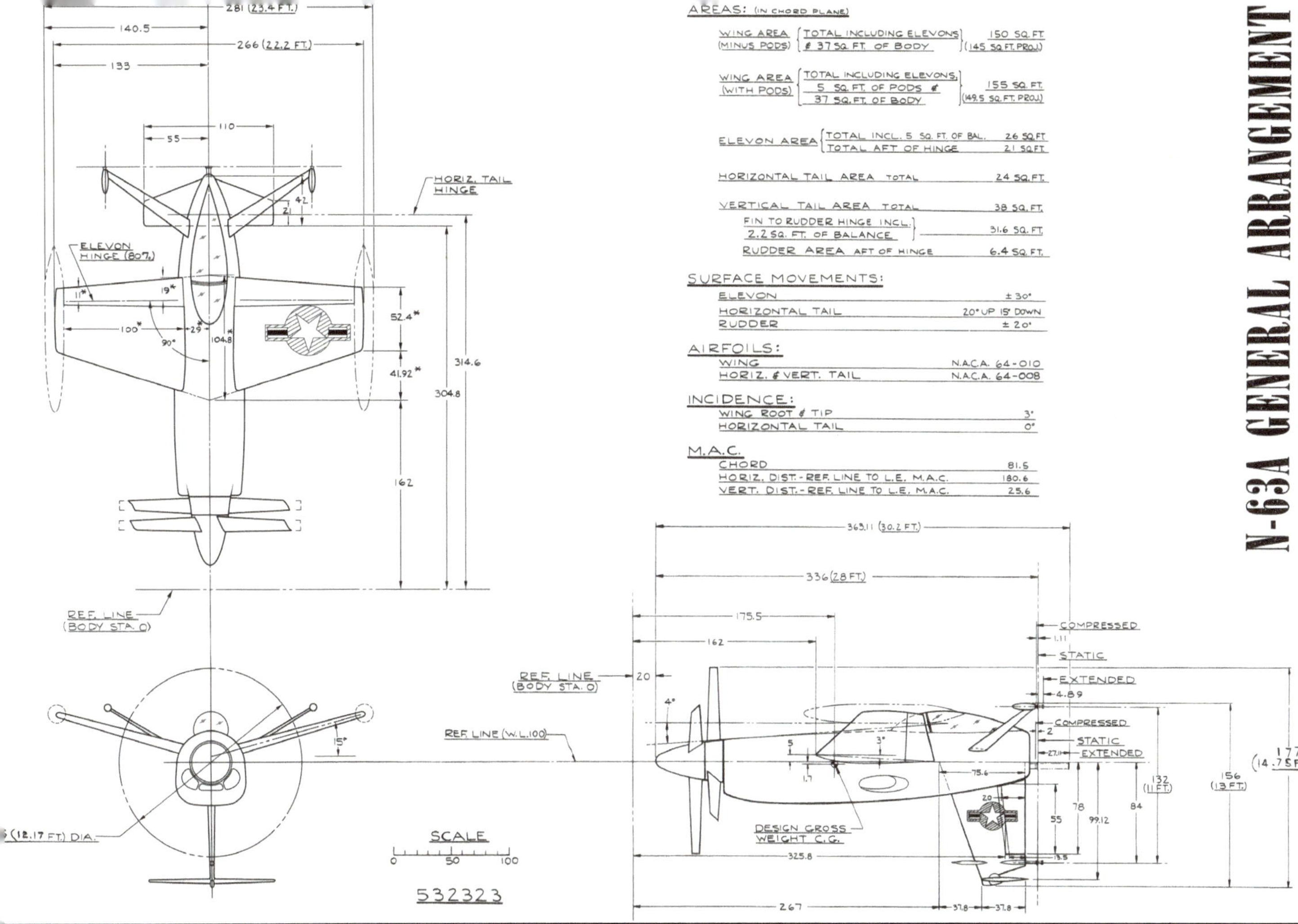

N-63A GENERAL ARRANGEMENT

18) Artist's impression of a pair of Northrop N-63A tailsitters in flight.

19) An illustration of the N-63A just prior to touchdown on the deck of a merchant vessel; note the open canopy and tilted position of the pilot, both of which would have aided him in accomplishing these difficult landings.

20) A three-view of the Northrop N-63A configured for vertical takeoffs and landings.

21) Artist's impression of the N-63A undergoing engine removal and maintenance in a desert location. Maintenance could be accomplished with the aircraft either in the vertical or horizontal attitude, depending on how it was configured.

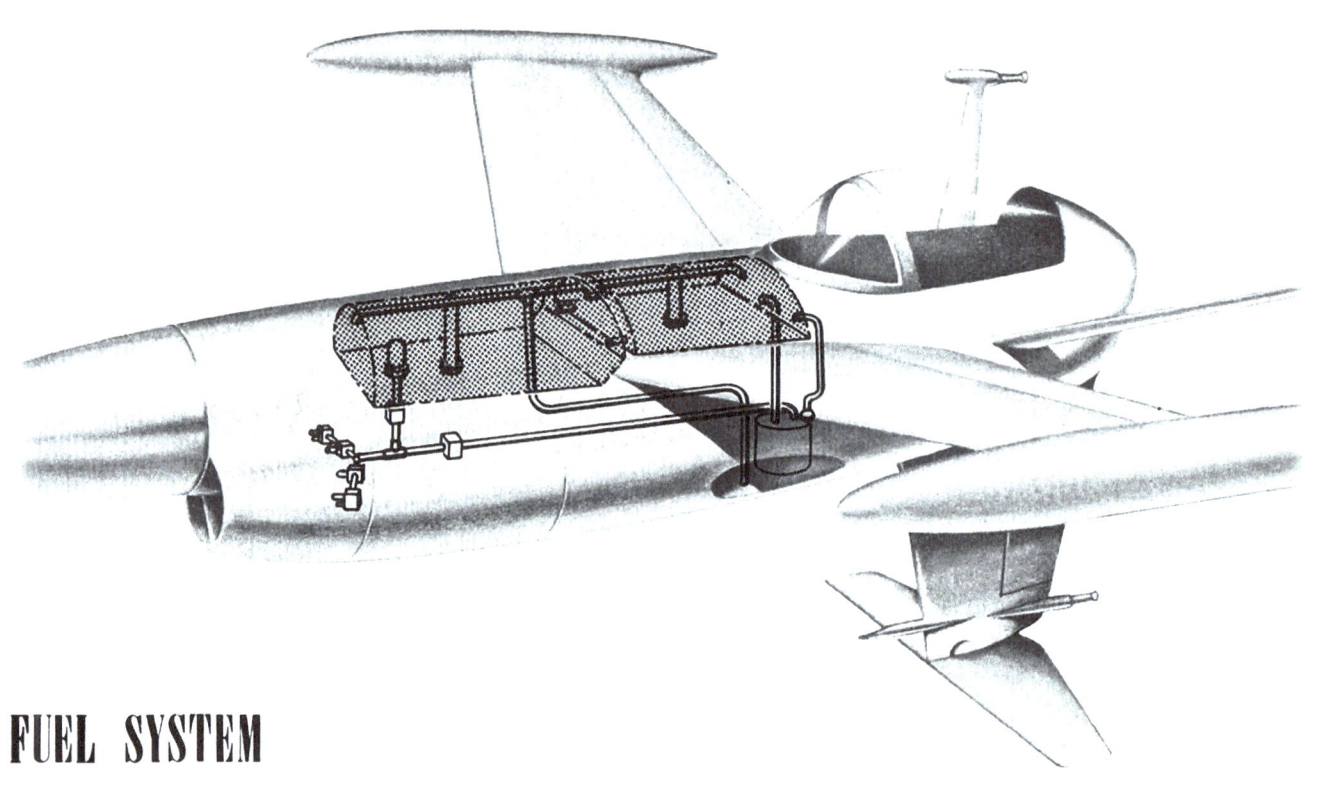

FUEL SYSTEM

▲ 22 ▼ 23

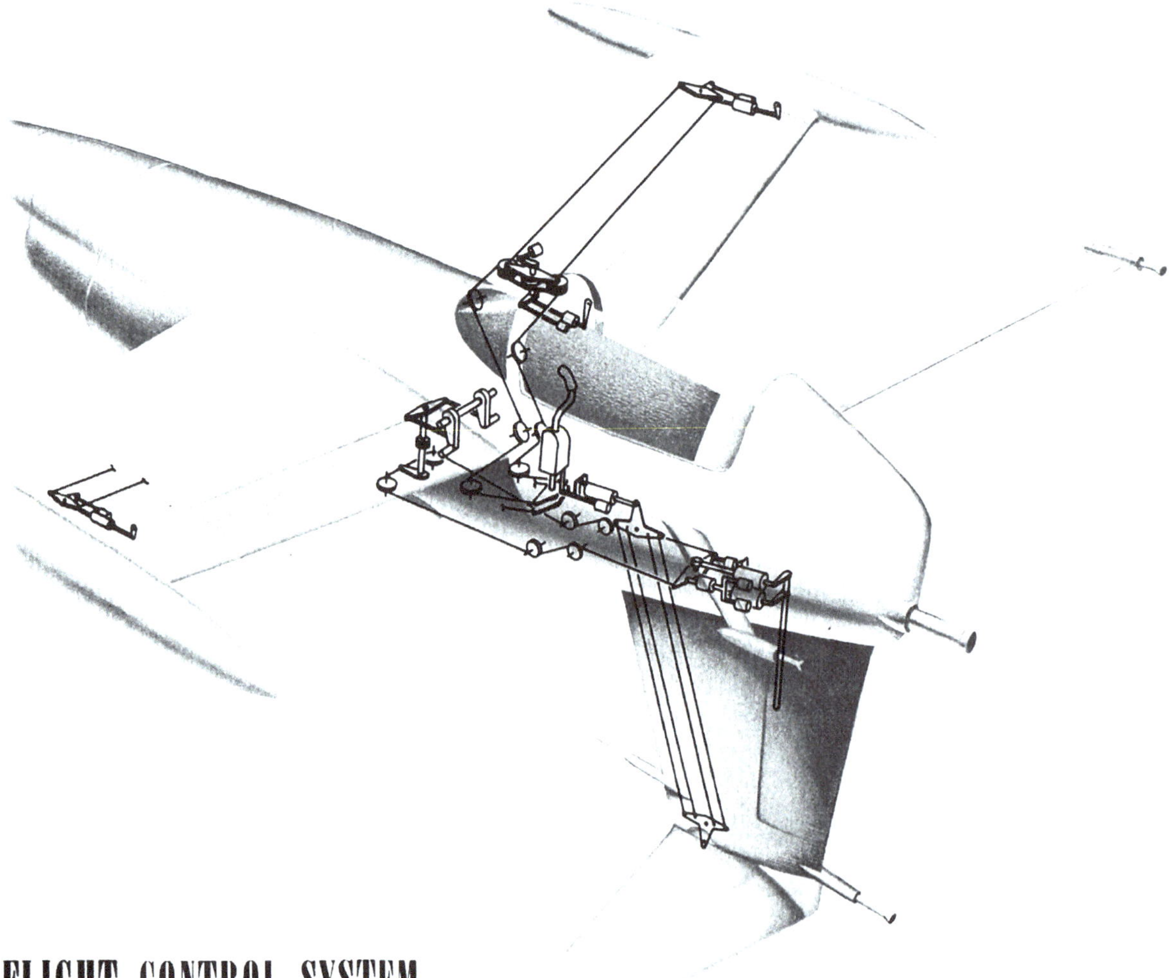

FLIGHT CONTROL SYSTEM

LANDING GEAR

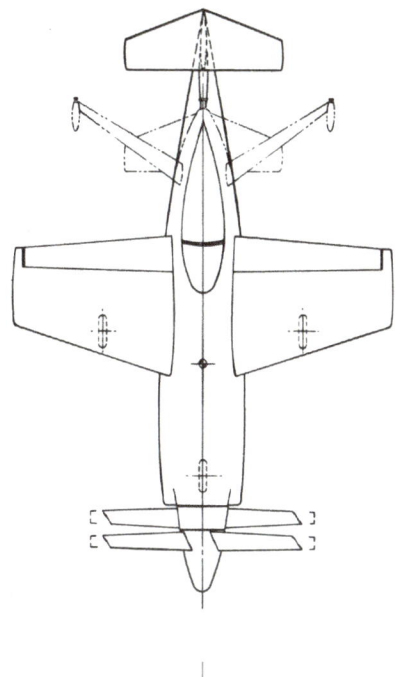

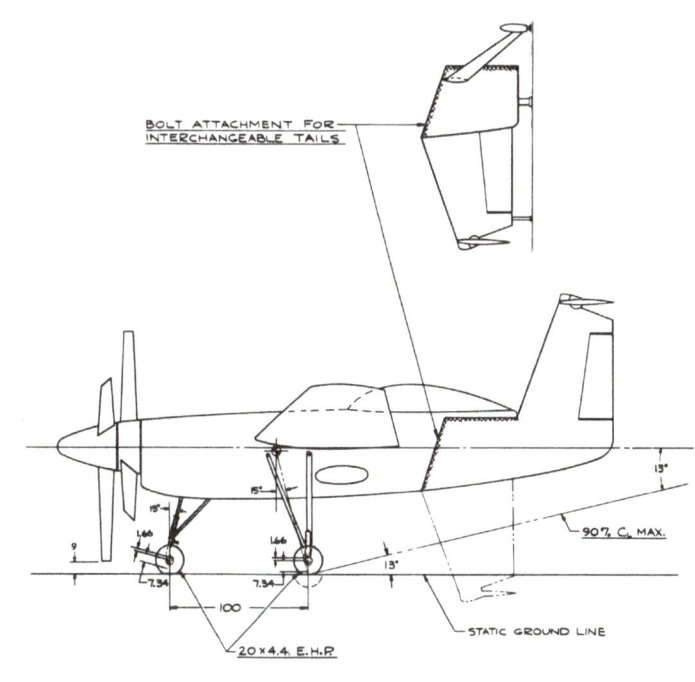

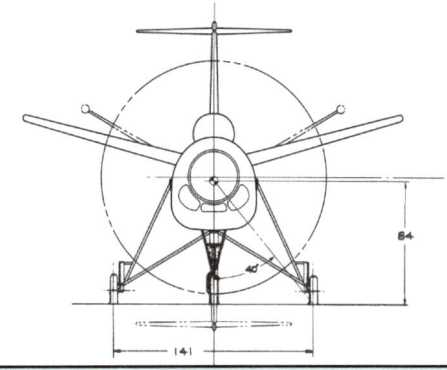

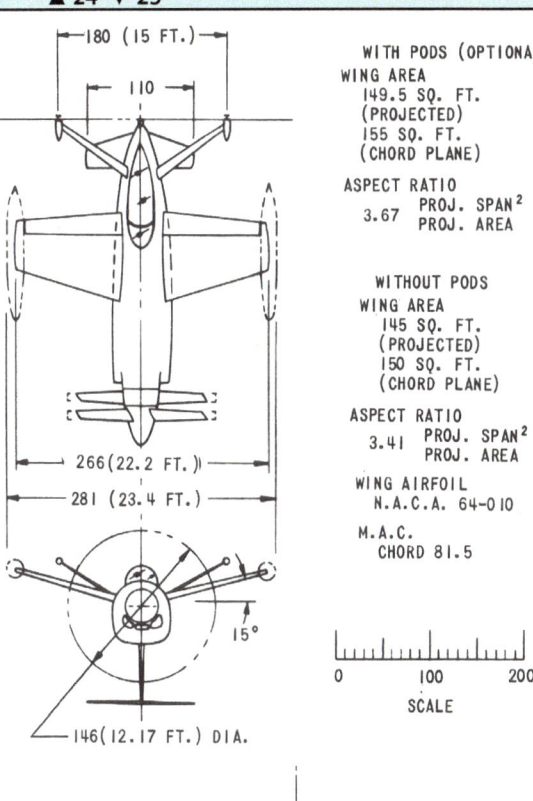

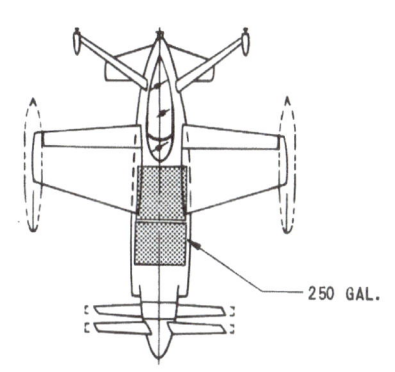

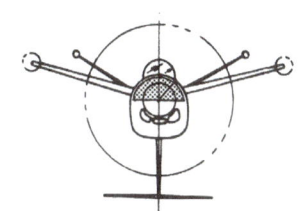

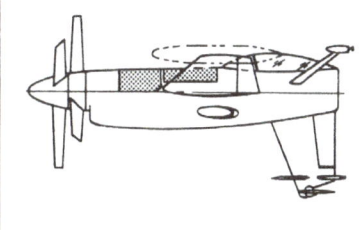

22) Diagram of the Northrop N-63A's fuel system, which had a capacity of 250 gallons.

23) Illustration of the flight control system for the N-63A configured as a tailsitter.

24) A three-view of the Northrop N-63A modified for conventional takeoffs and landings with a bolt-on tricycle landing gear and T-tail.

25) Three-view drawings of the N-63A taken from the Standard Aircraft Characteristics charts prepared for the type; the plan on the right shows the location of the fuel tanks.

26) Inboard profile of the Northrop N-63A scale prototype, which was powered by a British Armstrong Siddeley Double Mamba turboprop engine.

27-28) Standard Aircraft Characteristics charts for the N-63A. While the performance was not spectacular, it was sufficient to gather data on the feasibility of the VTOL tailsitter concept at minimal expense. Northrop would subsequently suggest abandonment of the N-63A in favor of a stripped down version of the full-scale N-63 to reduce the overall program cost.

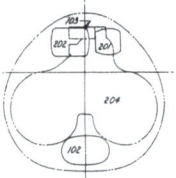
SECTION A-A

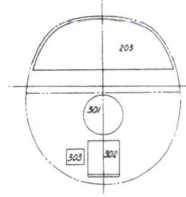
SECTION B-B

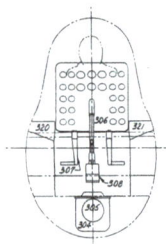
SECTION C-C

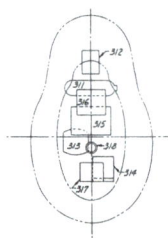
SECTION D-D

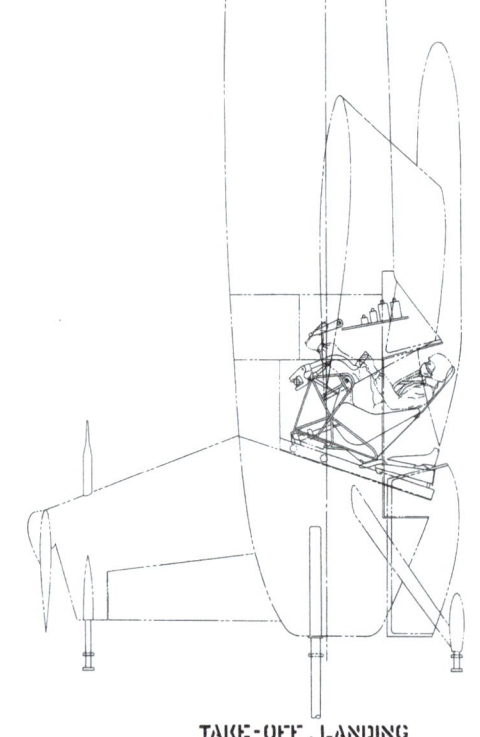
TAKE-OFF, LANDING & HOVERING POSITION

MISSION AND DESCRIPTION

The primary mission of the Northrop N-63A airplane is to provide flight research data pertaining to the U. S. Navy Class VF (Convoy Fighter).

The Northrop N-63A is a proposed U.S. Navy Class VF (prototype for Convoy Fighter) airplane based on BuAer Outline Specification OS-121. This prototype is an inhabited, flyable model, similar to the Northrop N-63, a U. S. Navy Class VF (Convoy Fighter) airplane. It is capable of vertical unassisted take-offs from, and landings on, small platform areas. It is also capable of performance indicative of the characteristics of the Northrop N-63 airplane.

The airplane is essentially a conventional single-engine tractor monoplane configuration except for features appropriate to vertical take-offs and landing. Longitudinal control at low speed and lateral control for all conditions are obtained by elevons, which also are drooped to improve ceiling and maneuverability. Longitudinal control during normal flight at higher speeds is obtained by an all-movable horizontal tail. Directional control is provided by a rudder on the vertical tail. Aerodynamic braking is provided by the propeller alone. The alighting gear consists of appropriate shock absorbers on two supporting members and the fin tip. Construction is all-metal. Crew consists of a pilot.

WEIGHTS

LOADING	POUNDS	L F
Empty	6,477 (E)	
Basic	6,543 (E)	
Design (flight)	7,785 (E)	7.5
Combat	7,785 (E)	7.5
Max. take-off*	8,465 (E)	
Max. landing	7,445 (E)	

* Limited by space

FUEL AND OIL

LOCATION	No.Tanks	CAP.
Fuselage	1*	250 gal.
Total		250 gal.
Spec.		MIL-F-5616
Grade		JP-1

* Not self-sealing

OIL

Capacity (1 fus. tank)		3 gal.
Spec.		MIL-O-6086
Grade		M

POWER PLANT

ENGINE

No. & model	(1) Double Mamba III
Mfr.	Armstrong Siddeley Motors Ltd.
Type	axial-flow turbo-prop.
Augmentation	None
Length (w/exhaust cone)	102 in.
Width	53 in.
Height	44 in.
Reduction gear	10.38:1
Specification	Installation folder Issue No.3

PROPELLER

Hub Manufacturer	Rotol
Blade manufacturer	Curtiss
No. blades/dia.	8/12.17 ft.
Blade design	No. 630-1C2 & 631-1C2

RATINGS

	Engine speed rpm	Shaft Power bhp	Jet Thrust lb.	Fuel Cons. lb/hr
Take-off	15,000	2640	810	2160
Normal	14,500	2095	710	1833

DIMENSIONS

Span	22.2 ft.
Length	30.2 ft.
Height	14.75 ft.*
Wing area	145 sq.ft.

* In horizontal position

ELECTRONICS

UNF Trans-receiver	AN/ARC-27
Radio Altimeter	AN/APN-1

N-63A INBOARD PROFILE

101	PROPELLER	13 FT. DIA.
102	OIL COOLER	
103	GENERATOR	

201	HYDRAULIC RESERVOIR	
202	OIL TANK	
203	FUEL TANKS	
204	ENGINE	DOUBLE MAMBA SERIES I
205	ENGINE MOUNT	
206	FUEL PUMP	
207	FUEL QUANTITY TRANSMITTER	

301	ENGINE FIRE EXTINGUISHER	
302	TRANSMITTER & RECEIVER	ARC-27
303	CONTROL BOX	ARC-27
304	FUEL PUMP & SUMP	
305	CONTROL FORCE BELLOWS	
306	INSTRUMENT BOARD	
307	RUDDER PEDALS	
308	CONTROL STICK	
309	THROTTLES	
310	EJECTION SEAT	
311	OXYGEN CYLINDER	295 CU. IN.
312	750 V.A. INVERTER	
313	HYDRAULIC RESERVOIR	
314	RADIO ALTIMETER	APN-1
315	AUTO-PILOT AMPLIFIER	
316	BATTERY	
317	HYDRAULIC PUMP (ELECTRICAL)	
318	LANDING STRUTS	
319	PITOT TUBE	
320	L.H. CONSOLE	
321	R.H. CONSOLE (ELECTRICAL) INCLUDES: ARC-27 CONTROLS, CONTROLS SWITCHES, CIRCUIT BREAKERS	
322	OXYGEN REGULATOR	

▼ 28

PERFORMANCE SUMMARY		
LOADING CONDITION		OUTLINE SPEC. OS-121 MISSION
TAKE-OFF WEIGHT	lb.	8,465
Fuel	lb.	1,700
Bombs	lb.	None
Wing/Power loading (A)	lb/sq.ft; lb/bhp.	58.4/3.21
Disc loading (A)	lb./sq.ft.	72.7
Stall speed - Power off	kn.	137
Stall speed - Power off - No. fuel	kn.	122
Stall speed - Power on	kn.	79
Maximum speed/Alt (B)	kn/ft.	405/S.L.
Take-off distance	ft.	0
Rate of climb - sea level (B)	ft/min.	6700
Service ceiling (B)	ft.	32,200
Time-to-climb ft. (C)	min.	
Time-to-climb ft. (0)	min.	
Vertical rate of climb (C)	ft/min.	5500
Absolute hovering ceiling (C)	ft.	7200
Combat range/V av	n.mi/kn.	
Combat radius/V av	n.mi/kn.	
Endurance at sea level/V (C)	hr/kn.	.75/0 .61/442

LOADING CONDITION		COMBAT	
GROSS WEIGHT	lb.	7785	
Engine power		Maximum	Normal
Fuel	lb.	1020	
Bombs/Tanks		None	
Max. speed at sea level	kn.	440	406
Max. speed/Alt	kn/ft.	440/S.L.	406/S.L.
Combat speed/Alt	kn/ft.	380/35,000	
Rate of climb at sea level	ft/min.	9980	7530
Rate of climb/Alt	ft/min/ft.	850/35,000	
Combat ceiling (500 fpm)	ft.	36700	
Service ceiling (B)	ft.		33,100
Service ceiling (C)	ft.	38800	
Time-to-climb/Alt	min/ft.		
LANDING WEIGHT	lb.		
Landing distance	ft.	0	

PERFORMANCE BASIS:

(1) NACA standard conditions.
(2) Calculated airplane and propeller characteristics; estimated and extrapolated engine characteristics.
(3) Endurance is based on Armstrong Siddeley Motors Ltd. Installation Folder. Issue No. 3 (dated March 1950) fuel consumption data using fuel of 6.8 lb/gal. (U.S.) density.
(4) Fuel consumption data are increased 5 percent.

NOTES

(A) Shaft power at sea level.
(B) Normal power.
(C) Maximum power.

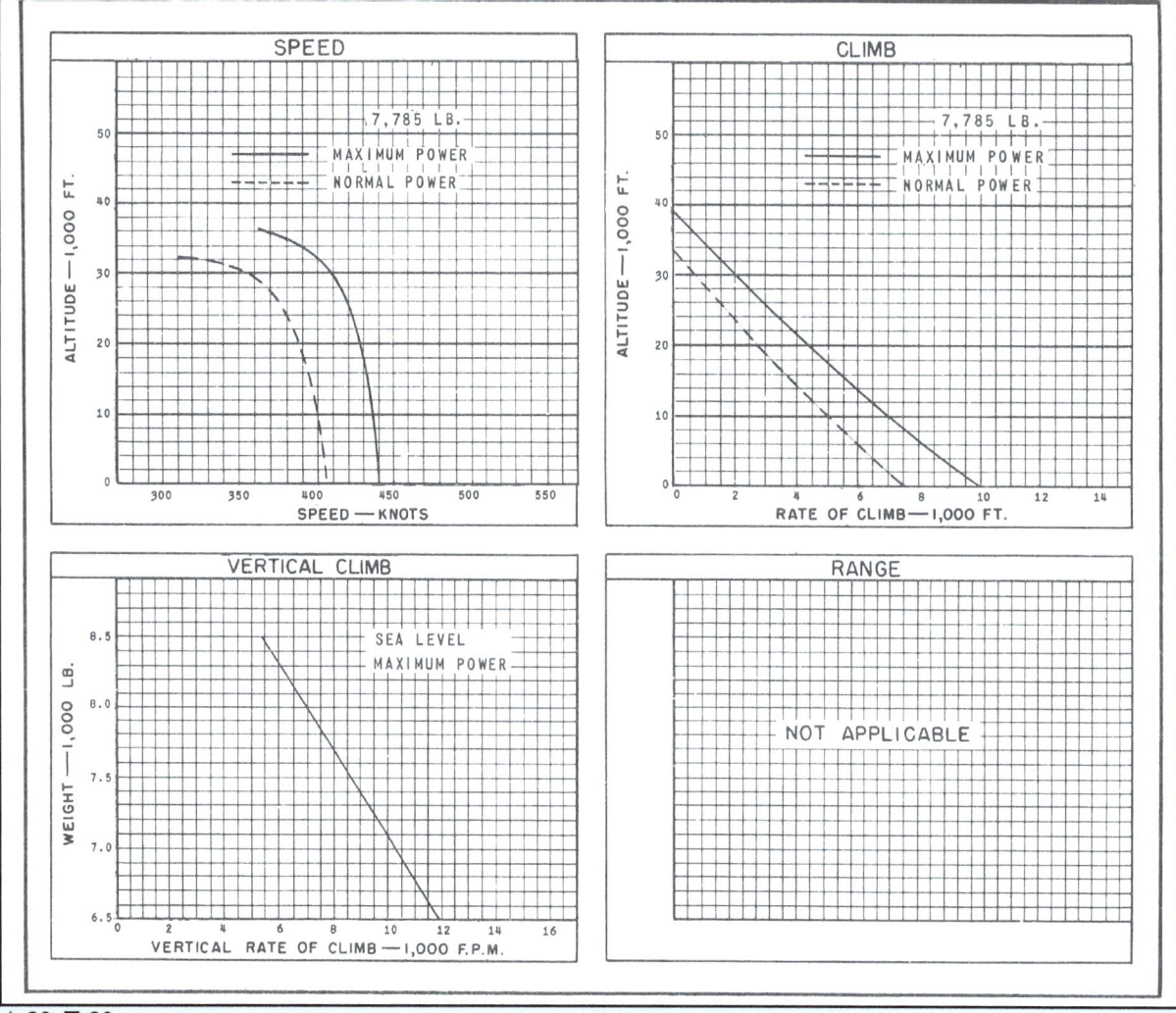

29) Performance graphs for the Northrop N-63A scale prototype.

30) Part of the cover to the cost proposal for the Northrop N-63 convoy fighter, which used the same artwork as shown on page 1 of this book.

Cost Proposal

Northrop's cost proposal for the N-63 was dated November 20, 1950, with additional cost information contained in a letter to BuAer dated November 24. The estimated total cost less fee for the Model N-63A scale prototype airplane was $7,103,153.92. (This and all subsequent figures are in 1950's dollars). This covered two complete flight articles; design data and structural tests; and demonstration. Northrop also proposed and recommended the following alternate programs:

1. A flight simulator was proposed in lieu of auxiliary horizontal landing gear and the auxiliary tail configuration required for conventional flight testing. A net saving of $727,831.40 would have been realized by use of the flight simulator.

2. Northrop also recommended an abbreviated proof test program, resulting in a net saving of $486,918.74 if this proposed test program was adopted.

The cost of the N-63 experimental convoy fighter was $9,463,929.20, which included two complete flight articles and one static test article; design data and structural tests; and demonstration. Northrop also proposed and recommended a proof test program which resulted in a net price increase of $1,271,034.69. This proposed program was based on a careful analysis of the test requirements considered necessary to ensure complete operational safety and proper system functioning prior to first flight. It had been Northrop's experience that full scale test stands were necessary for the development of power control systems, fuel systems, and power plant installation.

The combined total cost less fee was $16,567,083.12. The cost of the Northrop suggested alternate program was $784,115.95; this additional estimated cost brought the grand total to $17,351,199.07. The proposal was submitted on both a cost and a fixed-price basis; because of the unconventional, and there-

31) Northrop's proposed experimental fabrication and assembly layout for the N-63 convoy fighter.

32) The proposed experimental fabrication and assembly layout for the N-63A prototype airplane.

fore highly experimental nature of the program, Northrop was willing to undertake it only on the basis of a cost plus fixed fee (CPFF) or equivalent type contract. Accordingly, the proposal was based upon estimated cost without fee with the intent that the fee would be negotiated separately. Progress payments would have been required in accordance with contemporary CPFF practice.

Alternate Prototype. While Northrop was well aware of the logic behind the desire of BuAer to initiate the program with a scale prototype airplane, it recommended the following alternate program.

1. Informal studies indicated that an experimental prototype configuration using the full-scale N-63 airframe would provide test data and experience far more useful to the convoy fighter program than would the proposed N-63A, at an appreciable reduction in cost, time, manpower and material required for the overall program. The existing program involved the design of three rather different airplanes: an optimum convoy fighter configuration had to be determined; a tail-landing prototype had to be developed to represent aerodynamic characteristics of the fighter; and the prototype had to be modified to permit conventional take-off and landing, unless the proposed flight simulator was adopted.
2. All three designs involved separate and somewhat unrelated activity, including separate wind tunnel programs, autopilot developments,

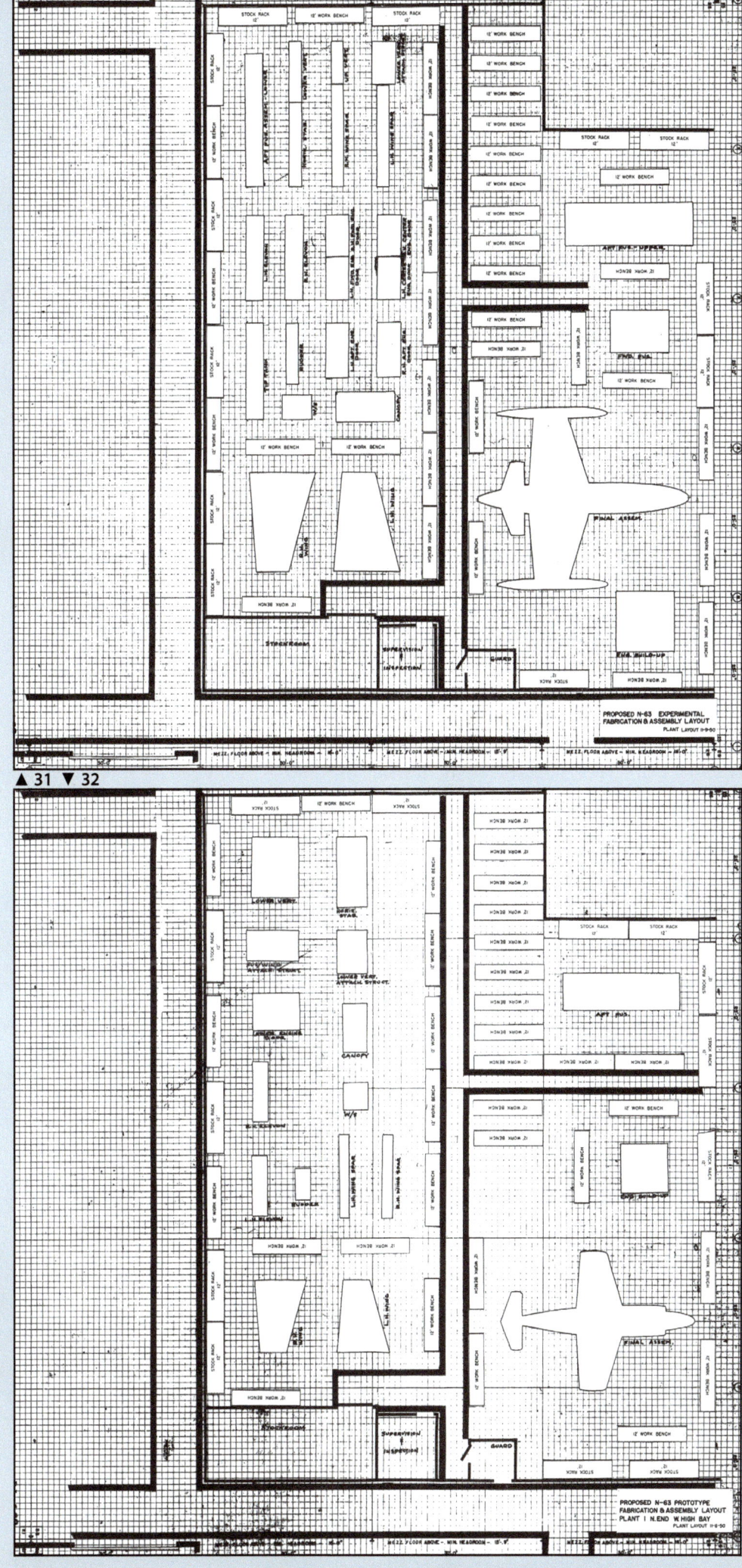

▲ 31 ▼ 32

proof test programs, manufacturing planning, tooling, and construction.
3. From a technical standpoint, Northrop asserted that the great advantage of a full-scale prototype lied in its direct applicability to the ultimate fighter design. Initial aerodynamic studies, wind tunnel tests, load analyses and autopilot design could have been conducted with a single airframe in mind. Similarly, design studies and drawings, manufacturing planning, tooling, and production learning would have been applicable to one airplane. Other savings to BuAer not reflected in Northrop's studies were the development of a single engine-propeller combination. Overall savings, for Northrop work alone, on the order of 25 to 30% ($4.5—5.5 million) appeared probable.
4. The advantages of using the full-scale prototype were summarized as follows:
   a. Northrop design of a single airframe instead of two or three.
   b. Direct applicability of wind tunnel, laboratory and flight test data to the ultimate fighter.
   c. Northrop procurement, tooling, and production for a single design.
   d. Navy procurement of the XT-40-A-6 engine, which was available at the time of the proposal.
   e. Navy procurement of the same two-speed gearbox for the prototype and experimental articles.
   f. Navy procurement of a single propeller, eliminating the need for a separate prototype propeller.
   g. Reduction in overall elapsed time for the complete program.
5. The disadvantage of the above was that the first prototype flight article would have been more costly than the first scale prototype flight article initially planned. This apparent disadvantage, however, would have been more than compensated by the elimination of the propeller and engine procurement costs for the scale prototype airplane. Informal studies were only made on the proposed alternate prototype airplane, with Northrop offering to submit a detailed cost analysis if the proposal was viewed favorably by BuAer.

Production Facilities. The Northrop Aircraft facilities were ideally suited for the production of an airplane of the size and type of the convoy fighter, as exemplified by the Northrop P-61 night fighter produced during WW II and the F-89 all-weather fighter which was then in production. The company provided BuAer with photos of these aircraft on the Northrop assembly line to illustrate their production capability.

33) Cover to the Northrop N-63 Progress Report No. 1 dated December 22, 1950.

Wind Tunnel Tests & Design Refinements

Northrop subsequently submitted an unsolicited progress report dated December 22, 1950 to BuAer, in which the company summarized its continued work on the convoy fighter design since the submission of its proposal the month before.

Introduction. During the period following submission of the Northrop convoy fighter proposal, the company continued preliminary design efforts directed towards refinement of the proposed configuration, and conducted wind tunnel tests with a low-speed stability and control model of the fighter airplane. Results of these efforts were informally submitted to BuAer, with the thought that they may contribute to the general fund of knowledge regarding this interesting problem. Northrop undertook these activities at its own expense, probably hoping to increase its chances of winning the convoy fighter contract.

Additional manpower and facilities planning, analysis of requirements, and establishment of project operational procedures continued, particularly with regard to preliminary design and wind tunnel programs necessary to the most efficient development of this unconventional airplane.

Design Refinements. Additional preliminary design studies of the proposed convoy fighter configuration had been concerned with minor design refinements. Detailed hovering stability calculations indicated desirability of some minor rearrangement of internal equipment and secondary structural components, in order to bring the center of gravity into closer alignment with the propeller thrust line. Accordingly, the changes indicated by the accompanying drawings and sketches were made. More detailed duct analysis and refinement of external fairings were included in these minor changes.

The changes indicated were expected to in no way affect the earlier estimates of cost or time for production of the airplane, but improve its performance and stability characteristics. External refinements were expected to improve top speed, although no estimates were made of the possible magnitude of improvement, pending more reliable propeller data.

Wind Tunnel Tests. The configuration tested in the wind tunnel produced data which were in excellent agreement with predicted characteristics of the proposed Northrop convoy fighter configuration.

The model was an approximate 0.16 scale model of the fighter airplane. Low speed tests were run in the Northrop wind tunnel to check basic aerodynamics regarding general stability and control characteristics, validity of applied theories, etc. Among the items studied were wing lift curve slope, wing and fuselage pitching moment, stability contributions of the propeller and horizontal tail, and drag increments of various components.

Test runs were made with various components of the model assembled in different combinations until the entire configuration was represented. Initial runs used the wing alone. Tip bodies representing the armament pods were then added. The basic fuselage was included in the next runs, without a propeller.

A windmilling counter-rotating propeller of the approximate desired characteristics was added next. Subsequent tests, as additional components were added, were run with the propeller both installed and removed. It was thus possible to establish the propeller contribution to the characteristics noted.

The ventral vertical fin was added for the next runs. This was then removed and runs were made with the dorsal vertical fin in place, after which both fins were installed for tests of their combined effects. Final runs were made with the horizontal trimming surface installed, completing the configuration.

As noted in the preliminary analysis outlined in the report, the tests showed excellent agreement with predicted aerodynamic characteristics. Purposes of the tests were completely satisfied by the indication of reliability of the general theories used in development

of the configuration. More detailed discussion of the results was presented in the report. It was Northrop's opinion, however, that the work so far accomplished verified the entire feasibility of design of a high speed vertically-rising fighter of the proposed N-63 configuration.

Summary and Conclusions of Wind Tunnel Tests. Northrop produced brief preliminary stability data from low speed wind tunnel tests of a simplified model of the N-63 airplane with windmilling propellers. The model differed in some details from the configuration of the airplane presented in the original proposal. The propeller blades used on the model were borrowed from another model, so they did not have the proper planform. No canopy or ducts were used on the fuselage. The vertical location of the wing corresponded to an advanced airplane arrangement which was completed after the convoy fighter proposal was completed. The flight surfaces had very simplified airfoil sections which were incorporated in order to speed construction of the model.

The results of the tests showed that the general behavior of the airplane and the stability contributions of portions of the airframe were very close to the predictions presented in an earlier Northrop report after corrections were made for the effect of configuration differences.

From these tests Northrop concluded that:
1. The horizontal tail size was probably margin-

34) Title page to the Northrop N-63 progress report which recycled artwork from the original November proposal brochure.

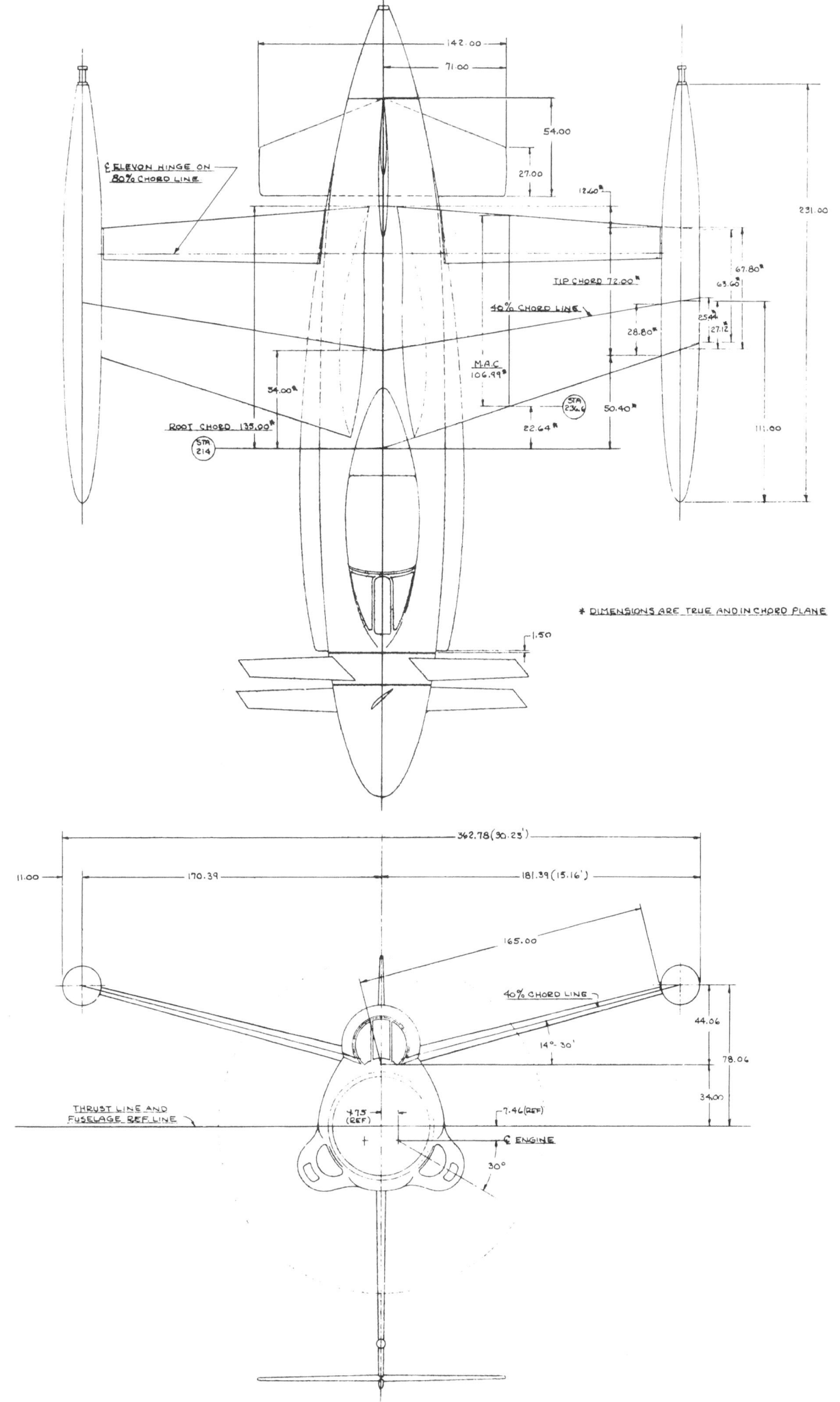

al, and an increase in size seemed warranted, subject to a study of stability and trim drag characteristics.
2. Although the values of the pitching moment coefficient obtained in the tests were not representative of the airplane, care was taken to obtain as small a value as possible.
3. Directional stability appeared to be somewhat too large, and a smaller vertical tail may have been adequate.
4. The effective dihedral of the complete airplane was larger than predicted or desired. The cause of this effect was not definitely isolated and further investigation was required.

Description of Tests. As part of the preliminary investigation of the N-63 airplane configuration, a series of wind tunnel tests of a simplified model was initiated. The model was designed to be rapidly built as quickly as possible and still yield data which were representative of the configuration. The data desired concerned only the stability and control characteristics of the airplane, and no special effort was made to obtain representative information on drag or stalling properties. The model had windmilling propellers with the blade angles set to correspond to high speed flight. This condition represented one of the critical conditions for both longitudinal and directional stability. Powered model tests were required to find the stability with

35) A comparison between this three-view of the N-63 from the December progress report and the one from the November proposal on p. 7 reveals several subtle changes to the design. These include a lengthening of the fuselage by 1.63 ft; an increase in the frontal area and volume of the fuselage; recontouring of the air intake fairings, which now extend much further aft; and a larger dorsal vertical stabilizer with rudder added.

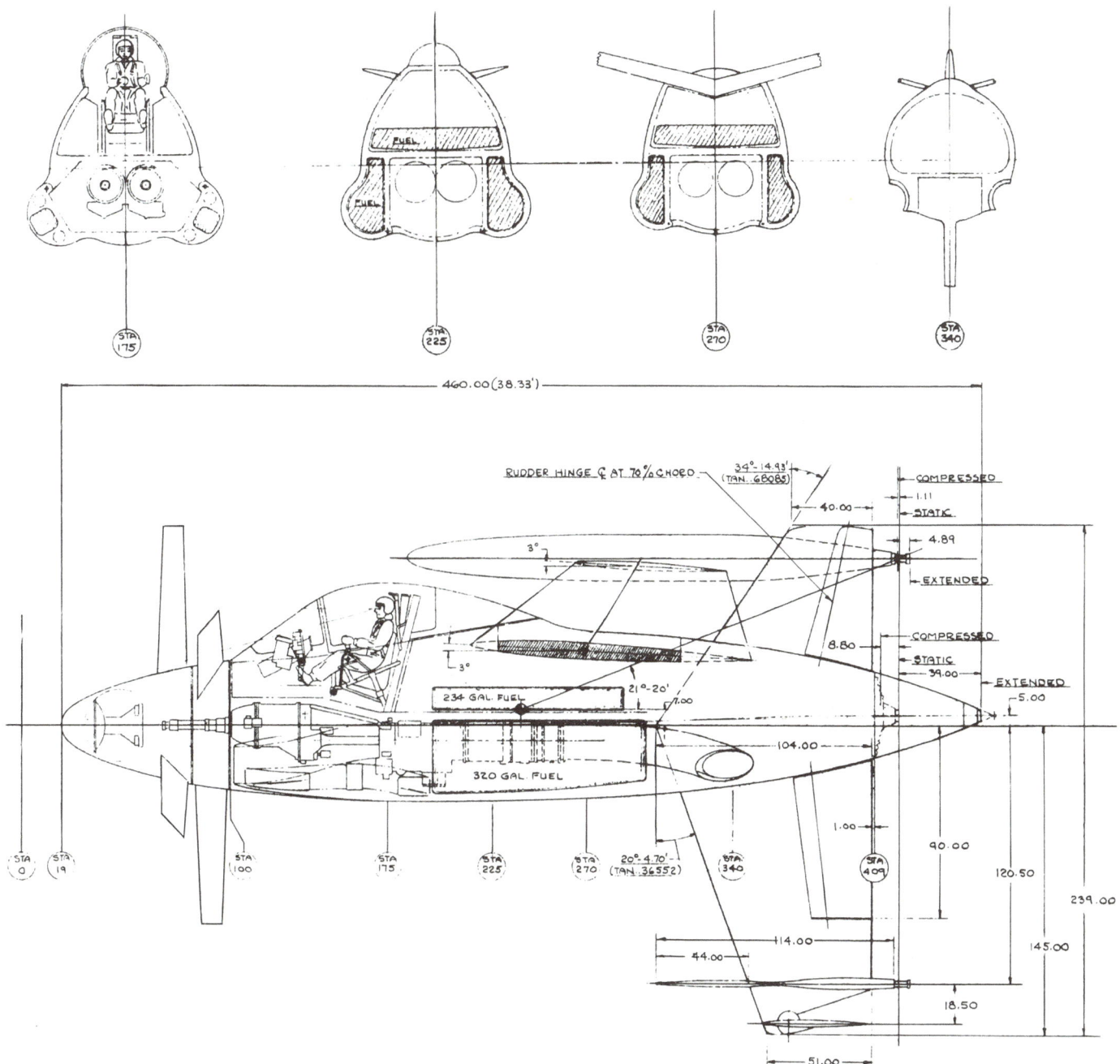

power on and to determine which conditions were most critical.

Tests were conducted in the Northrop low speed wind tunnel using the standard fork mount system. A special support system would have normally been desirable for this model, but this would have required lengthy calibration. The test period was December 5 through 21, 1950. The wind tunnel program and analysis of data were being continued in order to obtain a complete understanding of the stability properties of this aircraft type.

Model, Support System, and Testing Technique. A simplified model of the N-63 design was tested in the Northrop 10 ft wind tunnel. The fuselage consisted of a body of revolution and was constructed from laminated mahogany. A removable nose section allowed the testing of windmilling propellers or a smooth nose. Aluminum alloy propeller blades of the correct diameter were clamped in steel hubs to provide blade angle adjustment. The dual rotating hub bearings were lubricated with an air-oil mist to ensure consistent windmilling velocities.

An aluminum alloy plate was cut to the correct wing planform and bent to the correct dihedral angle. A constant chord bevel was made along the trailing edge on the upper surface. A leading edge radius of ½" was maintained across the span. At the wing mean aerodynamic chord location, the wing thickness ratio and camber corresponded with full scale. Consequently, at the root, thickness and camber were too small and at the tip were too large.

Tip bodies were turned from mahogany. These bodies had an elliptical nose, straight center section, and a straight tapered afterbody beginning at the wing trailing edge.

The horizontal and vertical surfaces were fabricated, in a manner similar to the wing, from aluminum and plywood sheet. Variable incidence of the horizontal surface was provided by means of a tongue and groove arrangement of the horizontal in the vertical. A slight amount of negative camber was incorporated in the horizontal surface section to prevent premature separation due to the subcritical Reynolds number of that section. The incidence range was -20° to 15° by five-degree increments.

The model was mounted inverted on the fork support system to minimize empennage and strut interference. Tare corrections to the data due to the interference of the supporting system were estimated from previous data. Consequently, the zero lift and zero angle values of the six components were somewhat arbitrary.

Corrections to drag and angle of attack due to wind tunnel wall effect were applied, but no correction was made to the tail contribution.

36-37) A simplified model of the Northrop N-63 convoy fighter, which was tested in the company's 10 ft wind tunnel December 5 through 21, 1950. The windmilling propellers were borrowed from another model and were not representative of those that would have been fitted to the actual aircraft.

Why Northrop Lost

Based on surviving BuAer notes, I believe the key factor in determining the outcome of the convoy fighter competition was weight. Northrop's estimated takeoff gross weight for the N-63 was 16,780 lbs. BuAer disagreed with this figure, estimating it to be 17,576 lbs, making it the second heaviest proposal in the competition after the Goodyear GA-28B. This excess weight reduced the estimated performance figures of the N-63, making it less appealing to BuAer. The eventual winners of the competition, Convair and Lockheed, were the lightest of the proposals submitted, with the former being the least heavy of the five contenders. That being said, all of the companies underestimated the takeoff gross weight of their designs to a greater or lesser extent according to BuAer analysts.

A second factor in the N-63's downfall was cost; at a total cost of $17,351,199.07, it was by far the most expensive of the proposals submitted, and this amount did not include Northrop's fee, which would have been negotiated at a later date. The second most expensive proposal was Lockheed's, which was quoted at just $12,403,188, fee inclusive. Martin and Goodyear's quotes hovered around Lockheed's amount, while Convair came in the lowest with an alternate program priced at just $4,756,741.40. Northrop was an expensive outlier in the convoy fighter competition, undoubtedly to its detriment.

Finally, Northrop had not landed a major Navy aircraft contract in quite some time, the last one being for the BT-1 dive bomber, 54 of which were ordered in 1936. In service, the type suffered from poor handling characteristics at low speeds and was prone to unexpected rolls, causing numerous crashes. While the BT-1 was eventually developed into the much more successful Douglas SBD Dauntless, the disappointing experience with the original Northrop design may have left a bad impression on the Navy that was difficult for the company to overcome.

▲ 36 ▼ 37

41

▲ 38 ▼ 39

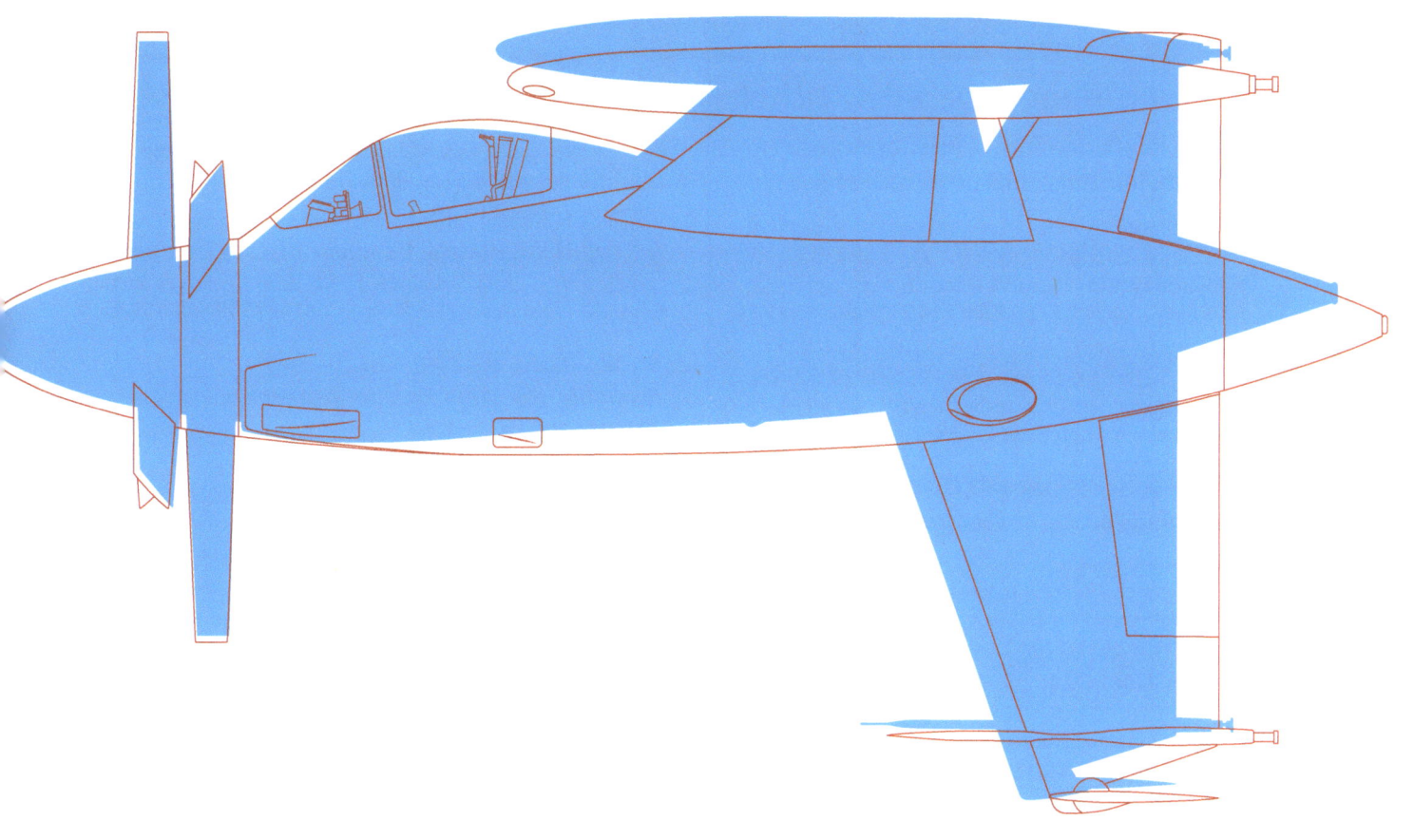

▲ 40

38-39) Aft views of the simplified N-63 wind tunnel model, which was constructed of mahogany, plywood sheet, and aluminum. It was designed to rapidly obtain data on the basic stability and control characteristics of the airplane at minimal cost.

40) A side view comparison between the N-63 configuration of November 6, 1950 (shown in blue silhouette) and the later one of December 22, 1950 (shown as red line work), both to the same scale. The December design was larger and more aerodynamically refined thanks to wind tunnel tests undertaken by the company.

Other Publications by Jared A. Zichek

Books from Retromechanix Productions
Available from Amazon.com & other booksellers

 **Goodyear GA-28A/B** *Convoy Fighter*: **The Naval VTOL Turboprop Tailsitter Project of 1950** Forty illos of a bizarre competitor to the Convair Pogo & Lockheed Salmon; 34 pp. **Print $14.99/Digital $5.99**

 **Martin Model 262** *Convoy Fighter*: **The Naval VTOL Turboprop Project of 1950** Fifty-six illos of Martin's proposed rivals to the Convair Pogo & Lockheed Salmon; 52 pp. **Print $16.99/Digital $6.99**

The American Aerospace Archive Magazine
Available at magcloud.com/user/jaredzichek

 **1. Martin JRM Mars Flying Boat: Commercial Projects of 1944** Reproduction of a beautiful full color brochure for a civilian version of the world's largest flying boat; 36 pp. **Print $9.95/Digital $3.95**

 **2. North American FJ-5 Fighter: A Navalized Derivative of the F-107A** Five wind tunnel model photos and 28 drawings of North American's unusual 1955 proposal; 36 pp. **Print $9.95/Digital $3.95**

 **3. The B-52 Competition of 1946...and Dark Horses from Douglas, 1947-1950** Seventy-seven rare images of early postwar strategic bomber projects; 60 pp. **Print $14.95/Digital $5.95**

 **4. McDonnell Naval Jet Fighters: Selected Proposals and Mock-up Reports, 1945-1957** 97 photos and drawings of early postwar jet fighter proposals & prototypes; 60 pp. **Print $14.95/Digital $5.95**

 **5. Mother Ships, Parasites and More: Selected USAF Strategic Bomber, XC Heavy Transport and FICON Studies, 1945-1954** Composite aircraft projects; 258 illos; 204 pp. **Print $49.95/Digital $9.95**

Books from Schiffer Publishing
Available from Amazon.com & other booksellers

 **The Boeing XF8B-1 Fighter: Last of the Line** Hundreds of rare photos, drawings, artist's impressions and manual extracts covering Boeing's last piston engine fighter; 376 pp. **$45.59**

 **Secret Aerospace Projects of the U.S. Navy: The Incredible Attack Aircraft of the USS United States, 1948-1949** Hundreds of rare photos and drawings; 232 pp. **$45.81**

Websites

Retromechanix.com Features hundreds of rare high resolution images and reports covering U.S. prototype and project aircraft from the 1930s through the 1950s. Many free and low cost digital downloads available!

www.ingramcontent.com/pod-product-compliance
Lightning Source LLC
Chambersburg PA
CBHW041124300426
44113CB00002B/57